The Survival of Helga Braun

Helga Braun

authorHOUSE®

THE SURVIVAL OF HELGA BRAUN,
by Helga Braun

"War is not healthy

for Children and Flowers

and other Living Things"

Who can better explain this ancient axiom than a small child who survived War? Helga is such a child, now grown to adulthood and living in the United States, and her story of War and Living Things sears the mind and stirs the heart. Her account is set in Germany during World War II and the early postwar years of national and personal reconstruction. If you have ever wondered what it was like in Germany during this period, or where was the humanity of the people living there, or if you seek a strong statement of the truth and a boost to your heart, then you will want to read this child's story.

It is not a story of the Holocaust whose depths of pitiful loss and horror can only be hinted by tears and silence. There are no doubt accounts more severe and heartrending than Helga's which is but one glimpse of the long story of uncounted millions of children, still struggling or long since muted, in the East and in the West, beginning from the ancient moment when War first raised its hideous head, through the millenniums to the present. Helga's is a simple account of World War II as it fell on the small shoulders of a helpless child, and how War's scourge slipped past the end of hostilities to continue its pain and loss through the present. Her entry into this life came in Germany, unfortunately with the rise of Adolf Hitler and his grotesque rally of hatred, conceit, prejudice and narrow-mindedness, that perversion of love we call nationalism. Trust and kindness, innocence and love, the flowers of the soul so evident in children, were crushed by War in the time of Helga's childhood.

For nearly eight years the Iron Fist ground flesh and bone and dear hearts, but little Helga somehow survived. From the child memory she now tells us what War is, very simply, sweetly, mercilessly, and what is the lovely Spirit of Life. No philosophical treatise, no dramatic sermon of the priest-craft, no impassioned speech of politics, can convey the truth of this child's story. When you read it you will want to reach back in time to console this lonely little figure, feed her, fend off her assailants and smother her eyes and ears from the cruel scenes of War. And you will want to reach into the future and the present to protect all children, the entire child humanity, young and old. Helga echos the silent cries of countless victims: we have only the present to be kind, to assure kindness – the forces of War, once unleashed, will run their brutal course. Our thoughts, words and deeds must acclaim the Unity of Man, of all Life, a unity which already exists at the level of the Soul, and a truth which is innately known by all children. We are all Men first, born the same way, constructed the same way, with the same privileges from God. The outer badges of creed and politics are man-made and should not stand in the way of our Unity. We must reject conflict and competition, and embrace the natural spirit of mutuality and cooperation. If we wish to end War and other scourges of our lives, we must follow the higher instincts of the child within us. For we, like little Helga, are all children of the Family of Life.

Helga Braun and Anne Frank are, in truth, sisters and would have dearly embraced.

(Book review written by Philip Anderson, a Vietnam veteran now working for the U.S. Department of Commerce as a computer systems analyst in Washington, D.C.)

First published in 1985
Vantage Press
Library of congress catalog No :84-91319

AuthorHouse™
1663 Liberty Drive
Bloomington, IN 47403
www.authorhouse.com
Phone: 1-800-839-8640

First published by AuthorHouse   6/21/2010

ISBN: 978-1-4520-2329-8 (e)
ISBN: 978-1-4520-2245-1 (sc)
ISBN: 978-1-4520-2246-8 (hc)

Library of Congress Control Number: 2010906593

Printed in the United States of America
Bloomington, Indiana

This book is printed on acid-free paper.

Special thanks to Imogene Warner and Dorothy Allison
for all their help on this book.
Especially for my husband, Tony, and my own beautiful children,
Sylvia, Angela, Tony, Jr., and Rick.

Children are a Gift from God. . .

To the Children—may they never see what I have seen
or live as I have lived

Contents

Foreword

My name is Helga Guariglia. I was born Helga Braun, the daughter of Adam and Lisa Braun, January 1940, in Mannheim, Bürgermeister Fuchs Strasse, Germany.

This book is the true account of my childhood memories from age four to eighteen. My story is not about dates or places, but the world of war as seen through the eyes of a child.

I have felt safe and secure since living in this country. Lately, however, reading headlines and seeing the unrest all over the world have brought back all the terrible memories of being a child living through World War II.

For years, friends and coworkers have urged me to write my story. Friends coming for a short visit would stay for several hours if I started to tell about my childhood. Coworkers listening at lunchtime would be late returning to work in order for me to finish telling a particular incident.

Maybe writing this book and getting it on paper will make it easier? Why did it all happen? Will it happen again? War is a terrible thing. It does horrible things to people and sometimes makes them animals. My children are all so innocent of my world as it was then. I don't think they could ever understand. I pray to God they never will.

The Family

My father, Adam Braun, came from a nice, respectable family. He was one of eight children, and his father, Karl Braun, worked hard to support them all. His mother died when he was fourteen years old.

Father had to go to work at an early age. He worked as an apprentice sheet-metal worker at the Mercedes-Benz plant in Mannheim. When he was sixteen, he met a girl at the plant and, against all his father's wishes, ran off and married her. The marriage lasted only a few months.

After the divorce, my father was disillusioned and left Mannheim. He was unable to get a job and probably too proud to go back to work with Grandfather, who had gotten him the job in the first place. I'm not sure exactly what he did or where he went, but sooner or later he went to Hamburg, Germany, where he met my mother.

My mother, Lisa Maucher, was from Hamburg. She was the daughter of a shipping merchant who dealt in silks and spices from the Orient. My mother was a beautiful, delicate, girl. She was only four-foot-ten and weighed eighty-six pounds. She had blonde hair and blue eyes. Mother had an older brother named Willi.

Both Mother and Uncle Willi had received fine educations. Mother had also been instructed in ballet since she was four years old; her brother, Willi, had been instructed in music. Both of their parents died in the year my mother was twelve years old and Willi fourteen. The courts put both children into an orphanage.

The entire estate once belonging to Mother's parents was awarded to the orphanage in which Mother and Uncle Willi were to be raised, leaving both Mother and her brother penniless. Mother stayed in the orphanage until she was twenty-one, and then she hired out as a cook. Willi was adopted at age fifteen.

Somehow, Mother and Father met, fell in love, and married in 1937, in Hamburg. Father brought Mother back to Mannheim in late 1937 and found a small apartment. Mother was pregnant.

It was about this time that the craziness spawned by Hitler began reaching its apex, and Father had to go into the German army. With Father gone, Mother found work as a cook at the restaurant "Liedertal." Momma was an excellent cook and soon made a name for herself in the kitchen. Because of her cooking ability she was able to work up to her very last month of pregnancy. During this time, Father would come home whenever he had furlough. Momma told me in later years that Father was never the same once they were separated and he had joined the army. The once outgoing, happy-go-lucky man she married had turned into a stranger. He did not trust anyone or get along with anyone, especially when he got out of the German army.

While this was going on, Hitler became more and more powerful. For those not carried along in his dream of pledging life and limb to the state, life was miserable. Even those who professed extreme dedication to his cause were still in fear of the SS.

The restaurant Liedertal was no exception. I remember an incident my mother told me about. It seems that one night, two SS troopers came into the restaurant. It was late. One of them demanded "Schweine Schnitzel." The waitress taking the order came back to the kitchen, her knees shaking, and told the head chef the request of the SS. She also told the chef that the SS trooper had told her the Schweine Schnitzel had "better be good or heads will roll."

Well, at that time of night, the restaurant was completely out of pork for the Schnitzel and it was too late at night to get more anywhere. The head chef knew this, and he was at his wits' end and scared. Usually, whatever any of Hitler's men wanted, they got. Even at this point, a lot of people believed that Hitler was made, but what could they do? To speak out against him meant certain punishment, imprisonment, or, worse yet, death. The common man simply tried to get along.

At this point, the head chef asked Momma for advice. She was scared, too, but finally she thought of something and told the chef not to worry, that she would take care of everything. Even though she was scared, she thought to herself, *If the SS wants Schnitzel, he will get a Schnitzel.* Momma thought to herself that no one had the right to act like that.

Everyone in the kitchen was relieved and willing to let Momma take over the responsibility of placating the SS troopers, although they didn't know how she was going to do it. What they didn't know was that Momma remembered a piece of pork that had been green and rotting and been thrown into the trash earlier in the day. When no one in the kitchen was looking, she casually walked over to the garbage can and quickly found the rotten pork.

With still no one watching her, she carefully washed the pork and scraped it to remove the green crust. She then proceeded to turn the rotten pork into a Schnitzel. First, she pounded and pounded the meat, which was only a small piece, the size of a small pork chop, until it was three times its size. Then she dipped the pork into flour, then into a mixture of eggs and milk, and then into breadcrumbs. Momma carefully fried the Schnitzel in lard to a golden perfection.

The waitress was so pleased when she saw that luscious "Schnitzel." Little did anyone know it was made from rotten meat from the garbage!

Everyone relaxed after the waitress served the meal and hoped the SS troopers would soon leave. However, it wasn't long before the one who had ordered the Schnitzel called for the head chef. When the chef heard this he was scared and just looked at Momma. She told him not to worry, that she would go out and talk to the SS.

The only reason my mother was willing to go out was that she figured they would not dare touch a pregnant woman. She was quite large at that point. So my feisty, four-foot-ten-inch mother marched out into the dining room to face the SS men. When she got there, the SS trooper that had ordered the Schnitzel asked "Who fixed this Schweine Schnitzel?"

"I did," Momma answered.

To her surprise, he handed her a large tip and told her that was the best Schweine Schnitzel he had ever had in his life. It was even better than his own mother's!

The entire staff was relieved! They had been watching everything from the kitchen door. Thanks to Momma, there had been no problem. With everything that was going on in the country at that time, everyone had been afraid for his life. After the two SS men left everyone congratulated Momma and took a deep breath. They would live. I don't know what ever happened to the SS man, but the Schnitzel incident became one of Momma's favorite stories!

Soon after that incident, on February 10, 1938, Mother had her first child, a son, my brother Helmut. Helmut weighed almost ten pounds at birth and had to be delivered by cesarean section. He was a good-looking baby boy, with golden hair and blue eyes just like Momma's. Her joy was great, but then the war really started.

The restaurant closed its doors, and Momma lost her job. She was pregnant again, this time with me. When I was born, on January 20, 1940, things were already pretty bad. Momma told me later how with all the anxiety and fears of the war, and the trouble she and Father had trying to keep food on the table, I weighed only three and a half pounds at birth. I looked like "a little worm," she once told me. I believe I was premature. I know Mother told me that the doctors in the hospital had to fight to keep me alive. Momma said that she was so happy when they finally were able to take me home.

I don't remember much about those early years, of course; everything I know is from what people told me later. The common people lived in fear of the SS and were being pushed into an unwanted war by Hitler. Father never once spoke about the war.

Hitler's motto was that you either did as he said or died. The German people could not even speak out for themselves. All that I can personally remember is an incident occurring toward the end of the war one day when Momma grabbed Helmut and me and ran just as fast as she could to a nearby bomb shelter as the shrill sound of the sirens was heard overhead. I remember Momma was holding me in her arms. Helmut was holding onto her dress. Hundreds of other people ran to the same bomb shelter. We managed to get there just in time as we felt the ground shake and the walls seemed to be moving. With every loud explosion, the crowd in the shelter moaned in fear. All the lights were out except for a few small ones, and they flickered on and off. Then there were more loud explosions. I could see the people in the shelter with us as my eyes got used to the dark. Everyone looked so scared. A lot of them, mostly children, started crying.

As we stood there and waited, and prayed, there was suddenly another explosion, almost on top of us. Debris from the ceiling fell and hit several of the people in the shelter. The entire ceiling looked as if it was going to cave in on us, but fortunately it held. As we looked up, though, we could see the steel beams emerging from the cement ceiling. As the bombing stopped, the screams and crying subsided. We were all alright, and we began collecting ourselves. I don't think I cried; I guess I really did not understand what was going on. There were only minor scratches on some of the people, where they had been hit by the falling debris.

When the sirens blew again, we left the shelter. It was the year 1944. I was a mere four years old. I remember Momma telling me and my brother Helmut, "Helga, now you two hold on tight to me," as we emerged from the shelter.

The Bombing of Mannheim

Hitler's prophecy "We will erase them" came back to haunt us, and the people who were saved by bomb shelters emerged to the most devastating sight.

I was four years old, going on five, and we were living in Mannheim when it was bombed. We had made it to a bomb shelter, and I remember that, on returning to Bürgermeister Fuchs Strasse, we found that our house had been bombed and was completely destroyed. All that we could save were a parrot and a radio. How the parrot lived through it was a miracle.

After the bombing, evacuation trains were enlisted to take millions of homeless people to the country, where they were put up in whatever shelter they could find. People lived in churches, stables, even pigsties. Anything—and everything—was pressed into service. We were lucky that my father took us to Colmar, a small city near the border of France, where a wonderful German farmer took all of us in.

Once we were settled in, my father soon returned to the German army, leaving my mother, my older brother, Helmut, and me behind with the kind farmer. Unfortunately for us, though, Father did not leave without leaving his devastating mark on Helmut.

I don't know how it all happened; I just know that my brother, Helmut, who was five or six years old at the time, had gotten into some kind of trouble with Dad. I'm not sure what I was doing that day when I heard my father screaming, "Helmut, where are you?"

The tone in my father's voice stopped me cold in whatever I was doing. I followed him and I could not help seeing the terrible events that followed. Apparently, Helmut had heard my father calling for him and, being afraid, had tried to hide. He was in the horse stable. On the way there, Father picked up a huge bullwhip, which had a large knot at the tip. I think the farmer only had it there for its looks, as I had never seen him use it, but when my dad picked it up, my heart stood still.

As we entered the stable, we could hear a sound coming from behind one of the stalls. I knew it was Helmut, and so did father because he said one more time, "Helmut, I know you are in here. Come out or else."

I think Father waited one more second, and then with a force I could not believe, he whipped the bullwhip over the stall where he suspected Helmut was hiding, and I heard the most awful, crunching sound but Helmut never cried out.

My father then ran behind the stall and I remember him carrying Helmut's lifeless-looking body past me and into the house. He had ripped Helmut's skull open with the bullwhip.

Since I was so young, I don't remember much of the events that occurred after that. From the stories the family told over the years, I do know that Helmut almost died, and it took months for him to recover from his injury. I think everyone was happy when Father left several days later to go back in the army.

Shortly after my father returned to the war, I can remember my mother telling me he had been injured. He had not been hurt in combat, but had been crushed between two trains while he was trying to connect them.

I don't know how long we stayed on the farm or for how long my father was in the hospital. We heard from him now and then, and his injuries were getting better.

Life on the farm was so different from city life; it was wonderful—like another world. My mother seemed to blossom for a while, apparently feeling free from the worry of war and all of the bombing temporarily forgotten. I could hear her laughing with the other maids while they were milking the cows. She seemed years younger and, oh, so beautiful then. Her blonde hair would curl around her face, her cheeks were red, and we were all brown from the sun.

Life for me was idyllic. All of the other children had to do chores, but, since I was so young, all I had to do was play. I can remember the farmer's wife calling me into the house and giving me freshly baked bread and milk. When Helmut came back from the hospital, he would play with me in the fields, where we would collect wildflowers. His injuries had healed fairly well; except for a huge bald spot, he was fine.

Helmut had to do chores, such as feeding the pigs, and the only trouble I had that summer was from Helmut, because he thought I should help him slop the pigs.

The only thing that would scare me was when the adults would get together to discuss the war. I would get frightened when I heard them talking about the enemy and how they were still coming across the Rhine River even though the Germans had blown up the bridges. Being as young as I was, I wasn't sure who or what they were talking about, but the seriousness of the talk, the tone of their voices, and looks on their faces scared me.

The Second Evacuation

The war was getting closer. My mother no longer smiled, and I seldom saw her laugh. It seemed as if everyone was preparing for the worst—and then it happened. Colmar was under attack, and we were evacuated again. Soldiers came in the middle of the night to evacuate us to Mannheim— where I had been born.

It was a cold, rainy night, and I still remember hearing one of the soldiers bellowing, "Hurry! The French farmers are coming after us with pitchforks!" I was terrified. The French claimed Colmar for themselves, and I thought they were going to kill us with large pitchforks like the one I had seen in the barn.

The soldiers loaded us onto a horse-drawn buggy, and we took off into the rain as fast as possible. We had only the clothes on our backs, and I was so cold, so very cold. Luckily, the ride was not long, and we were soon unloaded at the train station.

At the station, hundreds of people were already waiting to get away from the French border. Families were huddled together, crying, hungry, and cold. My mother was holding onto my hand so tightly that she was hurting me. I remember looking up at her and barely being able to see her face because of her big stomach (she was pregnant, but I didn't know it) and hearing her say, "Helga, we've got to get on that train. You must hold onto me or I might lose you and Helmut."

I held on, and, when we saw the train in the distance, she held onto Helmut and me even tighter. As the train got closer to the station, the huddled people became a howling mob, kicking and knocking one another down trying to get closer to the train and closer to escape. I was so small that people were stepping all over me, and I could hardly breathe. I was pushed harder against my mother. I could hear her groaning, and then a terrible thing happened—the crowd gave a big shove just before the train reached the station, and we heard a man scream, "No! No! Stop! My son fell on the tracks . . . please, please, get back!" Fortunately, I could not see anything, but I know now from the cries I heard that the boy and his father had both been crushed by the train as it pulled into the station.

I don't know how it happened—I think we were literally lifted by the crowd—but somehow we were on the train. Again, it was tightly packed. I guess I was lucky that I was small and could fit between people's legs, and, except for people standing on my feet, I could breathe.

It was terrible, though. Those inside the train next to windows were holding out their arms, trying to hold onto family members who were not able to get on the train, somehow hoping they could pull them in. Others outside the train were hanging onto anything they could—hoping to be carried to safety.

Finally the train was moving, and the people inside cheered. They had made it! Now they would live! Little did they know what was in store for them further down the track.

As the train began moving and picked up speed, I either fell asleep or passed out. When I finally awoke, I was still standing on the train, holding onto my mother's legs, with Helmut holding onto both of us. I don't know exactly what woke me; maybe it was hearing my mother moaning, but I was just in time to see the most incredible thing: My mother was having a baby! She had to squat to make it possible, and I remember seeing her reach down and take the baby, a boy, who was all bloody, into her arms and put it inside her dress, trying hard not to let the people next to her crush him to death.

Then it happened. I heard the airplanes overhead and the sound of bombs exploding! It was an awful sound! As the train was hit and came to a stop, I could hear the people screaming. The screams are something I can hear to this day.

Fortunately, our car was not hit in the first wave. Everyone jumped off the train and hid wherever they could find cover. My mother—with the baby still inside of her dress—Helmut, and I hid behind the car we had been riding in.

I don't know how long the attack lasted; all that I do know is that except for the car we were hiding behind, the train was completely destroyed. We were all shocked and could not believe that the enemy could be so ruthless as to bomb a train full of evacuees, but today I am convinced that those pilots did not know who was on that train and that they believed it to be full of German soldiers and supplies.

When we were sure the planes had left and the bombs had stopped falling, my mother looked around and said that there was a town in the distance, and that we would have to walk there. As we got up from the train, she said something that I thought very strange at the time, "Helga, Helmut, close your eyes, hold onto my coat, and just keep walking." It made no sense to me, why should I close my eyes in the broad daylight?

Oh, dear God, I didn't listen to her, and I wish now that I had. I can still see the scene all around me: what appeared from a distance to be only a man's coat, but actually still contained an arm in one of the sleeves; a woman, holding her young one, who was missing both legs. Everywhere I looked, I could see people's clothing, hats, shoes, and metal from the train. The debris was strewn all over the countryside.

As we walked toward the town in the distance, my mother kept telling me to keep my eyes closed, that we would be there soon. But, to someone my age, it seemed like a very long time. It was snowing again, and I was so tired, so cold, and so scared. Once, when I looked back, I saw a trail of blood in the snow. It was coming from my mother. I realized now that it must have been the afterbirth from the baby, but then I just remember praying, "Oh, please God, let my momma be okay. Please don't let her die."

I don't know how long it took us to reach that little town; it may have been an hour or it may have been a day. When we finally got there, it appeared to have escaped the war. We were directed to a nearby church that had been converted into a temporary hospital. Doctors and nurses were caring for the people who had managed to make it there from the train.

They had tried to divide the church into little cubicles, which were separated from each other with screens or blankets to provide some privacy, but it was almost impossible. There were just too many people. I can still remember the chaos and confusion as more and more refugees came streaming in.

After what seemed to be a long wait, a doctor finally saw my mother. I remember a nurse telling me not to cry, that my mother would be out soon. She was right. The doctor took only a few minutes before he ushered her out of his temporary office telling her, "The priest is right down there, behind that curtain."

My mother found the priest behind the curtain and all I remember hearing the priest say was "I christen you 'Gerhard Braun.'"

A short time later, little Gerhard was dead.

My memory fails me after that. I don't know what happened to little Gerhard or what he died of. I did not see him buried, and I do not know where his body is, but he is still in my mind and my heart.

After we were all looked after, my mother tried to get us transportation back to Mannheim; it was impossible to find a job there, and we had to have a permanent address so that Father could find us after the war. We had Father's address, but his hospital was quite far from where we were. Since Momma's brother, Willi, and his wife, Rosel, lived in Mannheim (as did Father's family), she decided that was where we would go. If any of our relatives were still alive, we would find refuge with them.

We could not find any means of transportation, so Momma decided that we would walk. I remember that it was late in the year, it had already snowed, and it was very cold. It was October or November of 1944, and Momma told us that she would like to be back in Mannheim by Christmas.

Momma did not know how far it was to Mannheim or how long it would take us to get there by foot. It had not seemed far when we went to Colmar by train.

I was very young then, but I can remember Momma's face as we started off on our journey; her eyes were red, and the laughter was gone. I don't remember my mother ever laughing again the way she had while we were in Colmar. Helmut had changed too. He didn't pick on me or tease me as he once had. He became very protective of me and held on to me wherever we went.

I can't recall much of the conversation that took place as we made the trip to Mannheim. But I do remember walking from town to town and hearing my Momma beg for food or try to get a temporary job so we could get something to eat. When I got older, they told me that we had walked from the train wreck to Offenburg, to Pforzheim, Karlsruhe, Bruchsal, Heidelberg, and then to Mannheim, a total distance of roughly 350 km. Somewhere along the way, someone had given us a little homemade wagon and a blanket. Momma put me into the wagon so that I did get to ride a part of the way. I'm sure she did it because I was so little and my legs were so short that it must have made slow going.

We were not the only people on the road. There were hundreds of other refugees going in the same direction. If it rained or snowed, we would try to find shelter and stop for a while, even if it was just under a tree. At night, we found whatever shelter we could. We did not always stay on the roadways; sometimes we had to walk through fields, meadows, or through forests. I can still see the bodies of those who had died along the way; whether from hunger, cold, or injuries, I didn't know, but they stayed where they had fallen.

Momma had to put me into the wagon more and more, because the soles of my shoes had worn through or come off in the front, exposing my toes. She tied a handkerchief around my shoes to keep them together, but soon the handkerchief wore out. Finally, Momma just tied rags around my feet. I remember it was getting colder, much colder than the day we were evacuated from Colmar. I don't know about Momma's and Helmut's shoes; I guess they were in the same condition as mine.

I especially remember the day before Christmas; the wind had become very cold, especially as we moved through the open fields and meadows. Even though I slid way down into the wagon and pulled the blanket around me, I was still chilled to the very core. Sometimes, the rain made the blanket wet, and we would hang it on a tree branch to dry. But now that it was so late in the year, it was harder and harder to dry our belongings.

It had started to snow again, that Christmas Eve, and there was no town in sight. We had walked quite a while already. I believe several days or weeks had passed since the train wreck. Momma had been able to get a few crumbs of food here and there. One day, she got a job cleaning a barn, for which she received three potatoes. We had no way of cooking them, so she put them in the wagon, beside me. Helmut and I finally ate them, raw and dirty, peel and all.

As we walked along, the snow started to get worse. Momma was crying, and the snow collected on her eyelashes. By then, I was almost stiff from sitting in the wagon. Occasionally, Momma would stop, and she or Helmut would shake the snow off my blanket; then we would move on.

It was getting dark, and we were covered with snow when finally, we came to a small farm. I heard Momma beg the farmer to let us stay in his barn. He made us welcome and said that there were already several others in the barn, that we should go ahead and make ourselves comfortable.

Momma brushed all the snow off us before she pulled our wagon into the barn. There were about eight other people there, all dressed in long, black coats just as we were. They appeared to be two different families. One couple had one little boy; the other had two boys and one girl. They paid little attention to us as we found a place in the straw. It seemed as if the farmer had fixed up the barn for them or for other people, refugees, like us. The others seemed like good people.

As we settled in, Momma took off my long, black, homemade stockings and hung them to dry on a nail. She then rubbed my feet until they started to hurt. I had not felt them before, but, when she rubbed them, they started to feel very funny. She did the same with Helmut's and her own feet. Then she put some rags on all of our feet to keep them warm until the stockings were dry. She had also hung up our coats.

There was a small fire burning in the barn, away from the straw. I heard the farmer telling Momma that we'd better be careful with the fire and to tell the others the same. He had put it in there for the refugees only.

Momma told me to move around a little to get back the circulation in my feet, which I did and they soon began to feel better. As we settled down,

I could see through one of the large cracks in the barn door. It had begun snowing quite heavily. I looked around the barn then and realized that the rest of the people there looked miserable and hungry, just like us.

As we sat there, the barn door suddenly opened, and the farmer came in, carrying a large bucket full of steaming hot turnips and red beets. Everyone jumped up and gathered around the farmer and his wife, who was behind him, holding a lantern. The room came to life, and the excitement was great! The farmer wished us *"Frohe Wheinachten"* (Merry Christmas), and he and his wife left.

One of the men divided the turnips and red beets equally among all of the people in the barn. When Momma brought us the hot food, it was as if she had come back to life. After we had eaten, Momma started to sing:

"Stille Nacht,
Heilige Nacht"

which translated into English means:

"Silent Night,
Holy Night"

I had learned the words the year before. As we sang, the rest of the refugees joined in. After singing "Silent Night," the others sang some other Christmas carols.

When everyone quieted down, Momma told us that Jesus had been born in a barn, just like the one we were in. As I listened to the story of Christmas, I almost felt privileged to be there in the barn that Christmas Eve.

Suddenly, Momma stopped talking. She had seen something going on outside through the crack in the door. As she walked over to the door, everyone watched her, as I did. I started to get scared, but then Momma called Helmut and I over to the door, telling us there was something she wanted to show us. As I looked outside, I could see that it was very dark, except for the white snow. Helmut and I—and, I'm sure, all of the others—were extremely curious, especially when she said that God was going to send us a Christmas Tree, lit with thousands of candles to prove that he loved us; we would see it in the sky.

I believed anything my mother told me, and she was right, because suddenly, there, in the sky, we saw thousands of little lights, seemingly from out of nowhere. We saw them several times. Seeing those lights, I knew that God was watching over us, and I felt so good. I did not realize until years later that the miracle of our Christmas tree in the sky must have been flares sent up by either German or American troops.

I don't remember much more of our trip to Mannheim after that. I do know that we stayed in that barn for some time, with the farmer and his wife feeding us turnips and red beets. I guess that, when the snow stopped, we moved on with our little wagon. The farmer gave us some straw for the wagon, and I stayed a little warmer.

I do remember the sight that met our eyes when we finally got to Mannheim. Everything was in ruins and rubble. People were living under the most terrible of conditions, some much worse than we had had in the barn. As soon as we entered the city, we were told that we could not drink the water without boiling it first. Mannheim was beset with diseases and sicknesses, several of them fatal.

My mother pulled me past those bombed houses, not knowing they were soon to become Helmut's and my domain, scavenging for whatever we could find to stay alive. The first stop we made was at my Uncle Willi's house (my mother's brother and only living relative). It was a happy reunion, especially since my father was already there!

Back in Mannheim

We were back in Mannheim to stay, it seemed. Our only problem was figuring out how to survive. There was hardly any food in the stores, and everyone was living on coupons, which entitled each person to just so much, but we didn't have even enough money for that. Father could not get a full-time job because of his back injury; he could not lift heavy items or do heavy labor, which included the majority of the jobs available. In later years, he would come to work as a stoker in two different movie houses, a caretaker in a hospital, a sheet-metal worker, a gardener, and worker for the city which proved to be too hard for him.

From 1945 through 1949, however, he was unable to get enough work to keep us going, not that he didn't try. He would spend days looking for work, coming home beaten and disillusioned, only to go back the next day to stand in line for hours, just to be turned away again.

Even if we had had a lot of money, it would not have done us any good buying food. Everyone lived on coupons, and one person was allowed one-half pound of meat, 125 grams of salt, 20 grams of cheese, and I think, 2 loaves of bread, per week. Sometimes we sold our coupons because we did not have money to use them.

On June 20, 1948 the highly inflated *Reichsmark* was changed to the *Deutsche Mark*. I remember that just before it happened we paid almost 100 *Reichsmarks* just for one small *Brotchen* (roll). Now each person traded off his worthless *Reichsmarks* into 40 *Deutsche Marks*. Everyone started off equal. Now the German people could work hard and build themselves back up, but not us. Momma was sick a lot, we had a new baby, and Father's injury was keeping him from getting a job.

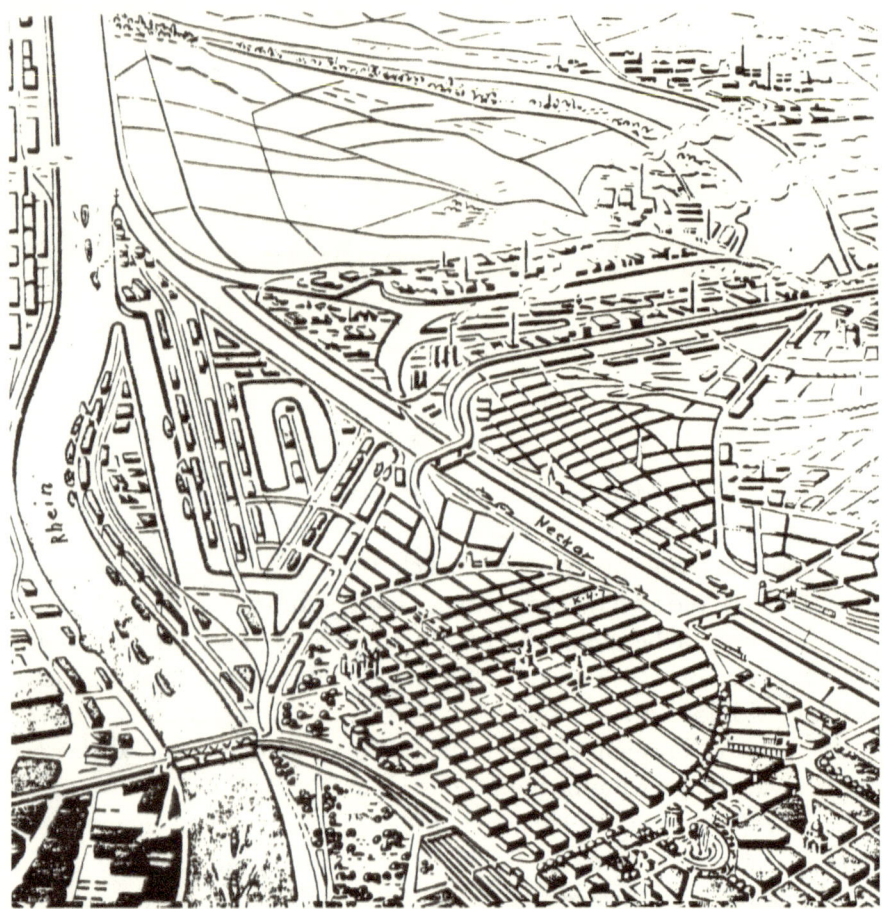

Helmut and I had to pitch in. We grew up fast and never really had a childhood in the normal sense. There were times I'm sure all of us wished we had died during the war, because in the years that followed we died a thousand times.

Uncle Willi and Aunt Rosel were fine. Their small apartment, which consisted of one room and a kitchen, had not been touched by the war. We stayed with them for a short time and then moved across the street into a three-room apartment. The address was K-4-7. The inner city of Mannheim is built like a horseshoe divided into city blocks. The blocks are identified by letters and numbers, such as A-1, A-2, A-3, up to A-7 or A-8. Following the block number is the house number, hence K-4-7.

Mannheim is nestled between two rivers, the Neckar and the Rhein. A high wall surrounded the city in the sixteenth and seventeenth centuries. It was built to keep out the enemy. Mannheim had been a fishing town. It had been founded by a man called Mano and later was named Mannoheim. Much later, it was changed to Mannheim. Mannheim had a beautiful water tower, surrounded by flowers and all kinds of statues. The water tower was still standing, as were all of our churches. The only damage done to the churches was that all of their windows were missing.

Momma belonged to the Catholic Church; Father was an Evangelist. I don't remember him going to church at all. However, as I grew up, I was taught in the Evangelist church, plus school every day.

Mannheim was now under American hands, and there were American soldiers everywhere. We had heard that the Russians were occupying Berlin and were raping women and young girls. The first time I ever saw an American soldier, I was so scared I started shaking. But nothing bad happened. As a matter of fact, they were throwing chocolate bars and candy at us. My fears soon disappeared. All the bad things we were hearing about the Russians did not come true with the Americans, at least not with us. I saw nothing but kindness in all of them. I remember a lot of the children my age started to beg for money from the soldiers. Most of the time, they got money or chewing gum. I begged, too.

Soon, however, the soldiers were not allowed in the residential sections or some of the residential bars, so we saw little of them after a while. The American government was very strict with their troops. Now you would only see them on main streets or on trains. They were always so neat and "spit shined." The Americans also had their own neighborhoods, where they could live with their families (this was not right after the war of course, but after everything had settled down), their own commissary, and their own hospitals and doctors. Soon you would see American cars shipped from the USA. They were the most unusual cars I had ever seen. I remember thinking that they looked like boats; they were so large and painted such funny colors. All I had ever seen were black cars or the kind that the police or rich people drove. Of course, there were very few rich people left at that time.

Even though I was too young to understand most of what was going on around me, I remember hearing the grownups talking and saying that Hitler had demolished many of the cities and things himself so the enemy would not get them. They used to whisper about how Hitler was a madman, and they hoped someone would kill him. You had to be careful about what you said, though, because a friend of ours who had talked about Hitler was picked up by the SS one day. We saw him after the war. His tongue was missing.

I also heard that anyone who would go against or say something bad about Hitler would be killed. The German people lived in fear of him. I had also heard about the Jewish people. We'd had neighbors, friends, and loved ones who were Jewish. Uncle Willi's wife, my Aunt Rosel, was Jewish; I believe that they told everyone that she was part German—part Gypsy. She was never questioned. Aunt Rosel was not from Mannheim, so no one knew about her or could turn her in. I don't know where her family was. She had married Uncle Willi before the war, and they had moved to Mannheim to be near my mother.

There was a lot going on then. Thank God I was only a child when all of it happened. Most of my information came from overhearing people or family talk after the war. By then, of course, it was all over. Much later, however, I heard that 19.2 million people had lost their lives by March, 1945. Two of Father's brothers were among the dead, along with countless people my family had known before the war. Our neighborhood baker and his family, who were Jewish, were gone. My family did not find out what happened to them until after the war. Most of the German people did not know what was going on, and, when they finally did, they could understand it even less, like the rest of the world.

We had also heard later that students from a university, on February 18, 1943, circulated fliers stating that the German youth would have to stand up against Hitler for themselves, or the German name would be ruined forever. Somehow it was found out that Kurt and Sophie Huber had been behind it, along with some other students who called themselves the "Weisse Rose." Kurt and his sister Sophie were sentenced to death on February 22, 1943.

There were others who stood up to Hitler: General Field Marshall Ervin von Witzleben was one of Hitler's most bitter opponents. He was hanged by the neck on August 8, 1944. Mannheim was one of the worst-hit cities in Germany, along with Dresden, Cologne, Berlin, and Hamburg—the birthplace of my mother.

So, here we were, back in Mannheim. We were home. Father had moved us into our apartment, and it was not too bad. Most of Mannheim was in rubble, but at least we had a home after all that walking. It felt so good to be inside a house. There had been about twenty houses on our block before the war; now there were only about twelve. The rest had been hit by bombs or were just unlivable. My father was lucky to get the apartment. Uncle Willi knew the owner.

The apartment was slightly damaged, but we did have a large stove, a large bed, and a table with two chairs that sat in front of a sofa. Only the middle room was furnished. I soon found out the other two rooms were rented to five other people. A couple and their two children moved into the back room, and a crippled lady in her twenties moved into the front room. We all shared the same bathroom facilities, which were in front of the apartment. There was one bathroom on each floor of the building.

My father was in charge of collecting the rent. I think that he charged the other people enough rent so that he had enough to pay for our share. Fortunately, also, Father had been able to select our room—the middle room—because it would be the warmest. It was also the largest. The back room had two windows; ours had only one. The front room had a small window too. The apartment was in the back of the building and had a courtyard in the middle. Not much sun hit our side of the building.

The couple in the back worked. He worked at night, and she worked during the day. The young crippled lady in the front worked too, but I guess she did not make enough money at her job, because Father soon found out that she was bringing men in at night to help pay her rent. We were not allowed to go through her room at night to use the bathroom, so we had to use a chamber pot, which was kept under the bed. The family in the back did the same.

Everyone tried hard to stay out of each others way. There were a total of nine of us in our apartment, not counting the men that would come and go in the front room. My father did not care about anything as long as the rent was paid, although I did hear him tell the crippled lady to try to get her boyfriends out of her room before we left for school in the morning. She was not too happy about the arrangement and moved out in early 1947, I believe.

With the woman in front gone, we started to have more problems, especially with the family in the back. The man had been injured in the war (he had been shot in the head), and he abused his children terribly. We tried to ignore it as best we could, but finally Father told them he would have to move out with his family. Now Father would have to pay all of the rent.

Strubele's Story

I was six or seven years old and was playing near the water tower, next to the train station—well, not really playing—I was "Kippen Stechen," finding cigarette butts for my father to get enough tobacco to roll a cigarette of his own.

As trains and streetcars pulled into the station, I would jump on and empty the ashtrays, then jump off quickly before the train left. I was thrown off by the conductor several times when I was not fast enough.

Sometimes, depending on the train, I would find enough cigarette butts for my father to be able to make two or three cigarettes. If American soldiers were on the train, they would give me a few cigarettes and maybe even some chewing gum or a candy bar.

One day, I got sidetracked, and found myself wandering over to the water tower. It was pretty there. There were flowers and vines, and even a waterfall, although it wasn't operating at that time. The main attraction, though, was the benches to sit on. I was always so tired, and it was nice sometimes to just sit and do nothing. All too soon I would have to go home, and it was a long way from Wassertum to K-4-7, inside the city, where we now lived.

As I was sitting there, I suddenly noticed a little dog, a puppy, smelling around the bushes. He was a mixed breed, coal black and fluffy, just like a butterball.

I very seldom saw a dog unless it was leashed. I could not believe my eyes! The puppy came over and looked at me with big, soulful eyes, and I reached down to pet him. Of course, after that he stayed with me, and, when he followed me home, I was glad for his company.

I did not think about how my father would react to the puppy until we got home. I was sure my dad would chase the puppy off, or even hurt him. We had never had a dog. I tried frantically to get rid of the puppy, but he would not go away. Finally, in desperation, I ran into the apartment, locking the door tightly behind me.

My father was in a bad mood as usual, and, when the puppy scratched on the door, I could see his face contort in anger. To my surprise, though, he let the puppy into the apartment. I told him what had happened and was amazed to hear him say that I had better keep the puppy in the house.

I said, "You mean that I can keep him?" He said yes and bellowed at my mother to give the dog some food.

She was dumbfounded! She looked at my father in amazement and asked, "What food? You don't mean the bread I was saving for breakfast?" I can remember her eyes going first to the puppy, then to my father, and finally to me. Then she gave the puppy the bread and did not look at me again.

I was so happy; I told my father he could have my bread for the rest of the day. I could not believe my luck. How could this happen? I had a pet! All that I could think about was how to feed him and to think of a name for him.

Although my father did not say a word, I knew we did not have any more food in the house for that week. Our ration for the month had run out, and there wasn't even enough for breakfast now.

The next day in school, all I thought about was a name for my pet. Finally it came to me, I would call him "Strubele," which means fuzzy, and that's what he was, a ball of fur. When I picked him up, though, I could feel nothing but skin and bones under all of that fuzzy black fur.

The Americans had brought an entire case of sardines to our school that day, and each child received one roll and a single sardine. It wasn't a lot, but I saved half of the sardine and a piece of my roll for Strubele. I was so happy, I ran all of the way home. Strubele almost went crazy when he saw me.

When I gave him the sardine, I expected him to just grab it and run. But not Strubele—he looked at the fish; then he looked at me with his big warm eyes, as if asking if I was sure. He then ate it. The rest of the evening, he never left my side.

I was so happy, but it seemed as if something had happened. No one was talking, not Helmut or the other families in the apartment. No one complained about the dog, not even the man in the back room, who was usually nasty and always complaining. I had been sure Helmut would be crazy about Strubele, but I was wrong. He never came near the puppy, and neither did anyone else. I didn't understand. I thought he was the sweetest, warmest puppy in the world. Not even Momma came near. In fact, she avoided him even more than anyone else. I put it out of my mind. I was just happy that he was mine; he loved me, and I loved him.

The next evening, when Strubele had been with us for two days, I was in my glory. I took him with me to the bank of the Neckar River to find coal that had fallen off the cranes when it was being unloaded from the ships. I found a few large briquettes, and, since I would not be going home empty-handed, I felt I could sit along the bank of the river and watch my Strubele run around a bit.

Strubele tired very quickly and sat beside me. As we sat there, I started talking to him. I don't know why, but words and feelings just started pouring out of me. I guess just knowing that Strubele liked me made me pour out my soul to him.

"You know, Strubele," I started to tell him, "the other day I was over at Annette Hilbert's house, she's the little girl from across the street. She was sitting on her daddy's lap and he called her his little princess and patted her hair. The only time my dad puts me on his lap is to beat me, and, Strubele, do you know that he never says he likes me? I sure wish I had a daddy like Annette." Strubele just looked at me and I went on.

"Did you know that Momma is going to have a baby in October? My dad really scares me sometimes. Do you know I saw him throw Mom on the floor and jump on her stomach with both feet, hollering all the while, 'I'll get rid of it! I'll get rid of it!' Momma begged him, 'Please, Adam, you are hurting me. Please don't!' I put my fingers in my ears so I wouldn't have to hear her cry."

Strubele was still looking at me, as if he understood. I looked him in the eyes and told him that I loved him and he licked my face. After that, it had gotten late, so we went home. When I went to bed, although hungry from having had only turnips for dinner, I was happy.

I can remember sitting in school the next day and thinking about that puppy of mine and all of the fun we would have that evening hunting for sticks of wood for the stove along the banks of the Neckar River. When school ended, I almost flew home, anxious to see my puppy. When I got home, he was not there to greet me. I called him.

"Strubele, Strubele, where are you?"

I searched all around the house; I looked everywhere but could not find him. Finally, my father said, "Stop looking for him; he ran off this morning right after you left for school."

I did not believe him and wondered if he had beaten Strubele. I didn't think my Strubele would run away from me. I wanted to go and look for him, but I was not allowed to leave the house until after dinner.

When Momma told us we would have rabbit, I was really surprised. We had not had any meat for many months. My spirits picked up as I ate some of the rabbit, thinking about the bones I would have for my Strubele.

I could not believe that hardly anyone else was eating the rabbit, not even Helmut. I was anxious to get all of the bones to save for Strubele. My father ate some of the rabbit and I got a few bones from him. I wrapped them in some papers and hid them under the bed.

When I was finally allowed to go out, I found Helmut, already out by the garbage cans in front of the house, his face ashen. He called to me, "Helga, come here."

I went over to Helmut, not suspecting anything, and looked into the garbage can. I can remember my entire insides retching. There lay my Strubele, his big eyes staring, the rest of his body gone, only the head and skin left. In a flash, I realized that I had eaten a part of my Strubele!

"Oh, God, let me die! What have I done?"

I started running and I ran and ran, trying to get away. Helmut was running behind me and caught up with me at the bank of the Neckar. He knew what I was about to do and grabbed my arm.

"Don't! Please don't!" he said and made me sit down beside him on the rocks.

"Do you want to die? Do you want us all to die? Mother and Father have not had any food for us for days now. I know a lot of the people in the area have eaten their dogs and cats."

"But why my Strubele?" I asked.

Helmut said the kindest thing I had ever heard. "Because he [Strubele] loved you, and now he is with God. He won't be hungry anymore. He gave his life so that you could live. I know that's how he felt."

I still felt like running, but where could I turn to? Strubele was inside of me; he would be a part of me forever and ever.

The Story of David

I can remember awakening one night from a bad nightmare and thinking that there was blood running down my face. I reached up to touch it and realized that it was more than a nightmare—there really was blood on my face. Apparently my screams from my nightmare had awakened my father and he had hit me in the nose to shut me up.

I had nightmares often. There were many nights I would lie in bed, afraid to go to sleep, afraid of the nightmares, and, worst of all, afraid of my father's beating me, should I scream.

In my worst nightmare, I dreamed about fainting on the street, being picked up by the sanitation department, and being burned alive. This resulted from the fact that several epidemics had hit our city and citizens were instructed to wrap their dead in sheets and place them on the curb. The city would then come by and pick up the dead for cremating. This kept the epidemic from spreading further.

The insane action of not sleeping nights, plus the lack of proper food, soon took its toll—I became nothing but skin and bones, with my stomach protruding. When whooping cough made its rounds, I was one of the first to get it. It is hard to describe whooping cough, but for days I felt I would die from coughing blood.

The people in town were talking about bad outbreaks of typhoid and Ruhr. After I had the whooping cough, my mother took me to a doctor. He told her I was suffering from severe malnutrition, anemia, and severe bruising of the kidneys. I also had extreme calcium deficiency.

I can remember that we had to wait about eight hours just to see the doctor. There were a lot of people in the waiting room, and I felt even worse looking around me. Some of the children looked like skeletons, and some had the worst boils I had ever seen. A woman who had been hit by a car passed out on my mother's shoulder. I remember my mother, my little tiny mother, trying so hard to hold the woman up so she would not fall on the floor. When it was our turn to see the doctor, my mother asked the doctor to take that poor woman first.

When we did see the doctor, he gave my mother some pills and cod-liver oil for me and told her she would have to exercise my legs since they were malforming. He also gave her a slip of paper that entitled her to get a pair of orthopedic shoes for me from the state. The pills and nasty-tasting cod-liver oil kept me hanging on by a thread.

Well, I did faint in the street on my way to school one day. Fortunately, instead of my nightmare coming true, it turned out to be one of the best days of my life, because David found me.

David was an American soldier who had been stationed in Germany. He found me lying on the sidewalk, and he picked me up and put me in his jeep. When I came to, I was scared to death to find myself inside of a jeep and next to a strange man. When I looked at his face, however, I felt safe. I remember he was young; he appeared to be in his twenties.

When he noticed me stirring in the seat, I saw a smile come to his face and, in the worst broken German, he told me that he was taking me home. (I guess he had found my address in my schoolbooks.)

It was a short drive, and we soon arrived at my house. When we got there, he lifted me gently out of the jeep and carried me into our apartment. I could not believe that anyone could be so gentle.

The American jeep parked in front of our apartment house caused quite a stir. I'm sure everyone that saw me must have thought that I was dying. Dying was such an everyday occurrence in our neighborhood. My mother was at the door to meet David, who had me still in his arms. She was crying, and tears were streaming down her face, wondering what had happened to me. She calmed down after I assured her that I had only fainted.

My mother pointed to a bed, and David put me down gently. He left soon after that, after trying unsuccessfully to tell my mother something. I was very sorry to see him go. I had never seen such a gentle man, and all that I knew about him was that his name was David.

To our astonishment, that evening David returned with another soldier and two bags full of groceries! The other soldier spoke fluent German. My mother thanked them for their kindness, and David told my mother, through the other soldier, that if it had been his child and the United States had lost the war, he would have wanted someone to treat his child the same way. We also found out that he was a medic and the father of two young children.

Mother thanked him again, and they soon left. The minute David and the soldier left, we immediately went through the sacks of groceries. We had never seen such food—there were cans and cans of food we had never heard of! I remember one, a can of creamed corn, because there was no such thing as edible corn in Germany (at least none I had ever heard of), and this was quite a mystery. We finally opened one can and tasted it. After eating, we decided that it had to be some kind of pudding or a delicacy.

Another item in the bag we had never seen was a box of Saltine crackers! There were just cans and cans of food, and we were very excited. We had peaches and pears and even potatoes in a can. What a miracle! I remember that we were amazed that these were in sealed cans, and I remember wondering how they got all that food into the can. We had to borrow a can opener from someone in the neighborhood.

There was also sugar, flour, and dried milk in the bags and several other things I did not understand. One of the most amazing things to me, though, was finding an orange. I had never seen an orange in my life! When my mother gave me one, I didn't know what it was or what I was supposed to do with it. Finally my mother told me to eat it.

Well, I smelled that orange, and I played with it, but I refused to eat it! It was so beautiful and smelled so good. Finally Helmut tried to take it away from me (he had been given a candy bar) and told me if I didn't eat the orange, he would!

When he said that, I ran off, and, as soon as he left the apartment, I hid the orange under my bed. I kept it for several weeks, only taking it out now and then to smell it or play with it. One day, however, I noticed that the orange had begun to deteriorate and was getting very soft. I finally decided to eat it and took a large bite out of it, skin and all. I didn't know you were supposed to peel it first. It was terrible, so soft and mushy, and, worst of all, it was moldy. I guess I had kept it too long. I spat it out and was very disappointed. Although it took me several years to eat another orange, the experience and the joy of just smelling the orange stays with me to this day.

Considering the rest of the food, though, it was as if it had been sent from heaven! From that first time, David would stop by about every two weeks and bring us some groceries. I came to look for him and not just for the groceries. I loved him dearly.

Then, one day, something happened. I didn't know what, only that I had contracted a terrible disease. Based on information I found out later, I'm pretty sure that I had typhoid fever, which had been occurring in epidemic proportions at the time. The only thing I remember is the terrible green diarrhea, the aching stomach, and the vomiting. On top of it all, I was still coughing from the whooping cough, and it was a blessed relief when my sickness made me delirious.

Thank God David was there. Since he was a medic, he was able to get me shots and medicine. David saved my life, and, because of that, I loved him even more.

While I was sick, he would come to visit and sit by my bed. I can still remember his soft hands as he would feel my head to see if the fever had broken. Thanks to David and his medicine, I was soon well again and even began putting on a little weight. My arms began to look normal, and my stomach, which had been protruding so abnormally, took on a natural shape.

It all seemed too good to be true, and it was. I saw the end coming the night my mother and father had a big fight. Father accused my mother of having an affair with David. I couldn't understand why my father was saying such terrible things to my mother. I knew she wasn't having an affair with David. David would always come to our house when he knew Helmut and I would be home from school and he and Momma would not even speak to each other. I knew that David came to see us and was helping us because of Helmut and me. I think that we reminded David of his own children and that he just wanted to be kind. I couldn't understand why Father had to ruin it.

The next time David came with groceries, my mother had one of our neighbors who could speak a little English tell David not to come back. I can still remember the look of disbelief on David's face when she told him. He apparently didn't believe her and came back with groceries once again. That time, Mother somehow managed to explain that my father would beat her if David came again. After that, he never returned. I remember the good-bye that day. David bent down to kiss me on the forehead, and I could see the tears in his eyes.

Now and again I think about David. Perhaps he will read my book. I hope so. David, if you should read this book, thank you, thank you. I still love you and thank you and all of the American soldiers that helped us and others like me. I think David would have been between twenty to twenty-five years old at the time, which is all I know about him. He would have been in the service between 1946 and 1948 in Mannheim, Germany, or nearby. I'm not even sure what branch of the service he was in; it could easily have been the army, navy, or the marines. I just know that he was a medic and an American and a wonderful human being.

The Junk Dealer

Everyone in the family had to work, since my father was making very little money and was not always employed.

At this time, my mother had a job cleaning bricks. She would get up early in the morning and go to a large building, where she would take a hammer and clean all of the mortar from the old bricks so they could be used for rebuilding the house. I remember she had to clean several hundred bricks to make enough money for flour for one loaf of bread. She would come home sometimes with her hands all blistered and bleeding, but she would just wrap them up in some rags and go back the next day to clean more bricks. The money my father earned was hardly enough to pay the rent or utilities. The only reason she stopped doing the work was that she got sick and pregnant.

At that time, it was scrap that would bring the best money: iron, glass, copper, lead, rags, and paper. Junkyards cropped up all over Mannheim. A lot of them were very dishonest, as I found out later. I can remember one junk-man who gave us presents and toys instead of money. At first, I was tickled about the nice jewelry box he gave me for quite a lot of iron Helmut and I had collected one day. Unfortunately, jewelry boxes could not buy food, and, when I got home, my father gave us both quite a beating, since there would be nothing to eat for dinner.

My father used to beat us quite a lot. I'm not sure just when the beatings began, but, after what he had done to Helmut, I did my best to keep my distance. What was so unreal about the beatings were that they seemed to occur for no reason. After what happened to Helmut, my mother was the next victim most of the time.

One incident I remember well. I had helped Momma set the table. She was especially excited about dinner that evening because we were having meat for the first time in weeks or months. The butcher shop had had horse meat and she had stood in line for hours just to get a quarter of a pound.

She had taken that small amount of meat and made a pot of goulash. She was so anxious for my father to get home so she could surprise him. She kept telling me, "Helga, see if he is coming."

I finally saw him coming down the street with one of the other men in the building and called to her, "Here he comes!" When Momma heard me yell, she rushed to the window. As Father came by, she gave him the biggest of smiles, she was so excited.

I was happy too and hoped that now we would have a nice evening. But that was not to be, because, when my father came through the door, he grabbed my mother and hit her with his fist, as hard as he could, several times. I could not believe my eyes.

My mother was also shocked, of course. She cried out, "Why are you doing this?" My father said, "Don't you ever smile at other men again!"

He was referring to the neighbor who had walked home with him.

My mother tried to explain. She told him he was wrong and about the meat and how anxious she had been for him to get home, that she knew how pleased he would be, but he would not listen. He was in a rage and was almost impossible to live with for the next few weeks. We all avoided him as much as possible.

Unfortunately, Helmut and I didn't leave him alone long enough, for one day we got into a small argument, as children do. We were outside of our apartment. All of a sudden, my father rushed from the apartment. He grabbed us both by the hair and dragged us inside. He first made me watch as he beat my brother with a foxtail, a hand sweeper made of heavy wood. I was so scared as I watched him beat Helmut that I peed all over the floor.

When he had finished beating Helmut, he threw him on the floor and grabbed me and threw me across his lap. I don't know how long he beat me, but finally, and fortunately, I passed out. When I came to, the doctor was bending over me with smelling salts. When he saw that I was conscious, he asked me what happened. Before I could say anything, my father answered, "She fell down the basement stairs, didn't you, Helga?"

He was standing behind the doctor when he said this, and I could see him holding up a fist at me as if he were going to hit me again. The doctor, though, could not see him. Of course, I told the doctor that what my father said was true.

The doctor turned around then and looked at my father. Then he told him, "Herr Braun, if your little girl ever 'falls down the basement steps again,' I will see to it that you spend the rest of your life behind bars."

After the doctor left, my father told my mother not ever to call the doctor again. I heard her tell him, "Adam, I thought she was dying." Well, from that time on, she never called the doctor again, but every time my father tried to beat Helmut or me, Mother got in front of us and took the beating for us. I'm not sure how many beatings she took.

I can remember one morning my Aunt Rosel came to visit. She was my mother's brother's wife and one of my mother's best friends. I overheard her telling Aunt Rosel that she could not go on living like this, and she told Aunt Rosel all about the beatings and that she had thoughts about walking in the river. I was so scared that I wished Dad would beat me and leave her alone. I told Helmut what I had overheard, and we made a pact that we would never beat our children, or anyone else, when we grew up.

My entire family lived in constant fear of my father. At times, my mother would have to stay in the house for days at a time to hide her black, bruised face. The neighbors all talked about us, but everyone was too scared of my father to report him to the authorities. I remember once, when a social worker came to our house, he almost threw her out of the window.

The worst beating I ever received happened one day when he sent Helmut and me out to hunt for scrap metal and told us that we had better not come home without money or else. It was late in the year, and we looked everywhere but could not find anything. It was getting dark, and I was scared and cold when Helmut showed me a house that was being rebuilt. I went in with him to find scrap. Usually, we looked only in houses that had been bombed and that were still in rubble. This house, however, looked as if it were being rebuilt. Helmut found some lead from the bathroom, and we hurried to sell it at the junkyard.

When we got home with the money, Father took the money, of course, and everything seemed to be all right, when there was a knock on the door. I answered it, and it was a policeman. He came into the apartment and told Father that he had a report from the owner of the old property that Helmut and I had been seen stealing brand-new plumbing.

Now, I had thought that lead looked new, but I was so cold, and it was getting so late, and I was afraid of getting a beating and going to bed hungry that I overlooked the fact that we had entered an off-limits property. We never, never knowingly took anything that did not belong to us.

My father told the policeman that he had no idea about our doing such a bad thing and, right in front of the policeman, grabbed me (I was standing closest to him) and gave me the worst beating. He told me, "I'll teach you to take stuff that does not belong to you." All the time this was happening, he had the money for the lead right there in his pocket.

Fortunately, the policeman stopped him before he went too far. By then, I no longer had any feeling in my legs. When the policeman finally left, my father said, "Well, we fooled him, huh?"

Well, he did not fool me. I was hurting all night and cried myself to sleep. From then on, I was very careful never to go near a house that looked as if it were being rebuilt.

The next morning, I could hardly get out of bed to go to school. My legs were stiff from the beatings and my toes stiff from the frostbite they had suffered while we were scavenging. I was really late getting to school and had to stand in the corner. At first I cried, but, as time went on, I could not feel my legs at all, so I did not mind standing there. Walking home was another matter. I was so glad Father would not get home until six o'clock and that Momma had time for me. She gently rubbed my legs and then soaked my feet in some salt water, which actually made them worse, but it was her loving care that was the real help.

While Mother rubbed my legs, she looked at me and said, "Poor Helga," which was one of her expressions. No one in my family ever showed much emotion except my mother. She told me that I was not to go looking for scrap that evening, but could stay home. At first, that sounded fine, but then I realized I would have to say home with Father. When I thought of that, I told Momma that I was fine and could go with Helmut to look for scrap, or coal, or whatever was needed.

Since money was the main problem that week, we looked for scrap. I walked out of the house with Helmut and pretended that my legs were fine. But once we got around the block, I started to cry and told Helmut about my legs. I know he felt guilty about the whipping I had received and he suggested that I go to visit Aunt Rosel. We went to her house, but she was not at home.

Helmut then suggested we go to the junkyard and that maybe the junk-man, Herr Mannes, would let me stay with him, while Helmut looked for scrap. I didn't know what to do at first, but, when it started to snow, I was all too willing to go. When we got there, Helmut asked Herr Mannes if I could stay there, and he agreed.

We had always likes Herr Mannes because, of our several junk dealers in Mannheim, he was the best. After Helmut left, Herr Mannes made me sit by the stove and gave me something hot to drink; it tasted like artificial coffee. It wasn't like Momma's, but it felt good and warmed me up.

While I waited, I looked around. Herr Mannes's home was just a shack held together by a couple of beams with scrap metal for a roof. It had no windows, just a door, and the walls were covered with newspapers. He appeared to have about two inches of newspapers on the walls, adding more each year as the old got dirty or sooty from the stove. The shack contained a table, a stove, two chairs, and a bed. It was about six by eight feet.

As far as we knew, Herr Mannes lived there, although I don't know if he owned the junkyard or not. I do know that he had lost his entire family, his wife, children, and parents, in a bombing raid in 1944.

Herr Mannes was a perfect example of a rough-looking person; he looked worse than my father. He was wearing a green jacket that once must have belonged to a fine gentleman. The jacket was made out of fine wool but was all dirty; the pretty buttons were all rusting and half were missing. The rest of his clothes were rather nondescript, but mostly I noticed his poor hands. He was wearing gloves, but most of his fingers came through the ends. I had not noticed it before, but his fingers were all mangled. When he saw me looking at them he quickly put them in his pocket.

I had to wait a long time for Helmut, and finally Herr Mannes and I started talking. He said very little about himself, so I told him about the terrible thing I had done the night before, all about the good plumbing and the beating. I also told him about my legs. As we were talking and I was telling him what happened to me, he was looking straight at me. I had never noticed what a nice face he had under his rough beard. He had warm brown eyes, and I remember them well because he looked as if he had tears in them when I was talking. The only thing that ruined his face was his mouth, because the poor man was missing nearly all of his teeth, and, when he smiled or ate, he looked rather funny. As we sat and talked, however, he became less and less ugly. I don't know how long we waited for Helmut. We had left the house shortly after getting home from school, which should have been about one-thirty, and now it was getting late. Herr Mannes kept me company between waiting on customers, like Helmut and me, who brought in scrap iron.

I remember one elderly lady who had pounds and pounds of old paper and cardboard boxes on a little wagon; another customer was a younger man with glass and tins. They all left in good spirits, because Herr Mannes treated them fairly as he did us.

As it got dark, I knew that Herr Mannes would close the junkyard at any time, and Helmut still was not back. I was afraid that I would have to go home without Helmut and without money. I didn't know how I would explain that I had done nothing all afternoon except sit at the junk man's shack. As I started thinking about how mad Father would be, I began to cry. I never cried so much in public except when someone was nice to me. For some reason, that had a bad effect on me.

As Herr Mannes started to close up the junkyard, I got ready to leave. When he saw that, he told me to wait a minute, that I couldn't leave without Helmut. "But you're closing," I said. He said, "That's all right, I live here. You can wait here by the stove."

Just then, Helmut came up the street. I could see that he was empty-handed. When he got there, he told us how the snow had made it impossible to find anything. I started to cry again and did not want to go home. But Helmut, who was much braver than I, said, "Let's go."

As we started to go, Herr Mannes stopped us and handed me one Deutsche mark. I looked at the money, and then at Helmut. I was dumbfounded. Then, Herr Mannes told us that it was just a loan and that when we had a good day and brought him some good scrap, we could pay him back. We just could not believe it! We could go home now; one Deutsche mark was enough money for one loaf of bread.

As we entered the apartment, Momma's face lit up, and she told us that she had been getting worried. Even Father seemed relieved to see us, and, when we gave him the money, everything was all right—we were safe for that night at least.

From then one, our friendship with Herr Mannes the junk-man grew. He had to wait a long time for his money, because, when it snowed, we had to spend our time finding coal down by the river, which was actually easier than finding scrap and making money. We would take two buckets each and watch for the cranes to unload coal from the ships. As they were unloading, coal would fall to the ground and we would run and try to get it before anyone else. Sometimes it was a little dangerous because a large piece of coal would hit you on the head or foot, but, other than that, it was easy to spot the black coal in the snow. There were always a lot of people there, but sooner or later you would find enough.

As soon as the weather broke, we were back to finding scrap. We were both anxious to pay back Herr Mannes. One day, we found a lot of scrap—almost two marks' worth. I told Herr Mannes that now he could keep one mark from the money as payment of the loan. Well, he said he had already held out his money! He said that we had brought in three marks' worth of scrap and that he was giving us two as he handed Helmut and me the money. Now, if there was one thing I knew, it was the price of scrap and how to read a scale. I knew that we had only had two marks' worth of scrap.

Herr Mannes winked at Helmet, and Helmut said thanks and "Let's go," to me. All the way home, I tried to tell Helmut how Herr Mannes was wrong and that we still owed him one mark, but, just like Herr Mannes, Helmut would not listen. He finally told me to shut up. "We have two marks; just be happy we have some money to bring home."

From that time on, I watched Herr Mannes's scales closely. Any time we had a really bad day, he would give us more money than we had coming to us, and he would never, never take it back. All I can say is, that wonderful man helped us so much, and, from that time on, Herr Mannes was included in all of my prayers.

It was early one Saturday morning and usually I would already be up and getting ready to go out looking for scrap. This morning, however, I did not feel good, so I just stayed in bed, pretending I was still asleep.

As I lay there, I heard Aunt Rosel come into the kitchen. She was saying "Happy Birthday," to Momma. "How old are you now, Lisa?" she asked.

Momma answered, "Thirty-six years today. Just imagine, I'm thirty-six years old and I feel like I'm sixty." The baby was due today also. Both Aunt Rosel and Momma thought I was still asleep as they went on talking. "You know, Rosel, I don't know how I can go on sometimes. Adam is just wishing the baby will be still born. I don't know how he can be that way—he is so cold and unfeeling."

Aunt Rosel just listened quietly and then she said, "I don't know how you can live with a man like Adam."

"Where would I go? What would I do? Besides, Adam has not always been like that. I remember before the war things were so different, but now, sometimes I think something happened to him in the war. He is all right one minute, then the next thing you know, he almost goes crazy. Have you ever seen the way he beats up on the kids? I don't think he really means to, but one of these times he is going to kill one of them. Do you remember what he did to Helga? I thought sure she was dead the way she just lay there

44

after he beat her. Helmut won't even cry anymore. I don't understand. No matter how hard Adam beats him, Helmut never makes a sound."

I had never noticed that about Helmut until Mother said that. Aunt Rosel told Momma, "Lisa, there must be something you can do. Adam almost killed you too, to get rid of the baby. Here you are nine-months pregnant. Adam just might get his wish yet. You are so little Lisa, your stomach isn't much larger than a small melon. Are you sure the baby is still alive?"

"Yes, I feel it kick. I just hope it will be healthy, I'm so scared he might have hurt the baby." Mother's voice sounded so desperate. I could tell she was in agony. Then she said, "Even if the baby is all right, I don't know if I am going to be able to nurse it. Not eating and all might dry me up before the baby has enough milk. There is just not enough food, Rosel. If it wasn't for Helmut and Helga helping, it would be even worse. I don't know how we can manage. Helmut and Helga are so little. It breaks my heart to send them out to work. Helga is so little. She's not too well. I'm letting her sleep late today. She's just a baby too; she is only seven years old. Rosel, how can God let this happen to us?"

By now, Momma was crying. Aunt Rosel tried to comfort her. My heart broke every time I heard Mommy cry, and there was nothing I could do. When I grow up, I thought, I will get a job, and I will have Momma leave Father and come live with me. I would make sure she would be all right. I prayed, "Dear God, let me grow up fast and make me strong."

Aunt Rosel soon left, and I pretended to wake up. I never said a word to Momma about what I had heard. I told her I felt good and got dressed and ready to go out to make some money. Helmut was already outside. Momma acted as if everything was all right when I left; she never let Helmut and me see her upset.

Helmut was getting ready to leave when I told him, "Wait for me," and we started off down the street. As we walked along, I kept hearing Momma's words, so I said, "Helmut, how come you never cry when Father beats you?"

Helmut stopped and looked at me for a minute; then he said, "The old man can beat me or do anything else he wants to, but he can never break me." I didn't know what Helmut meant by that then, but I do now. Mother was right about Helmut though. No matter what anyone did to him, he never cried. In years to come, I saw him cry only once, and that was when he was saying good-bye to Gela and me. His tears touched me more than I can say.

In the meantime, Helmut and I went to work. We worked as hard as we could. Knowing that Momma depended on us made it all worthwhile. I knew that if we brought home just one mark a day, it would mean the difference between eating and not eating, and, as Momma had said, today was her birthday, October 4, 1947. And the baby was due. Those two things made me vow to do anything I could. That day, we worked so hard, we even surprised Mr. Mannes with all the junk we hauled in. I had gone from house to house, begging for old paper or anything they had. We also had rooted around everywhere we could, trying to find scrap; we never stopped, not once, to take a rest. We made two marks that day, and the effort was worth it. Momma was very happy when we gave it to her.

"Gela"

My sister, Angela Rosel Braun, was born October 9, 1947, just five days after my mother's birthday. Her nickname was "Gela." Her middle name, "Rosel," was chosen for my Aunt Rosel. Aunt Rosel was always there for Momma, and they were very close. Fortunately, the beatings and kickings my father had given Momma during her pregnancy did not affect the baby. Gela was rather small when she was born, but otherwise she seemed all right.

I remember the day my mother brought her home from the hospital. She was so little. Momma was breastfeeding her. I was only seven years old at the time, and I was amazed at the sight, I had never seen a baby breastfeed before!

Unfortunately, Gela started to reject our mother's milk, and she developed terrible boils all over her little body. Momma went to a doctor, who told her to discontinue breastfeeding and to get a wet-nurse for the baby. When Momma told Father what the doctor had said, Father told her we could not afford a wet-nurse. I know Momma tried to find a wet-nurse, but finally had to give up.

She began feeding Gela dried milk, which we got from our church. Fortunately, the church was getting cases of the milk from the Americans. Gela did not do too well on just dried milk, and she soon became so sick that she had to be hospitalized. While she was gone, I missed her terribly, and Momma cried for her at night.

I'm not sure how long she was in the hospital, but Father finally brought her home when he and Momma found out they were not doing much for her there. As a matter of fact, the doctor had told Momma that Gela was dying. I remember Father and Mother proved the doctor wrong; they nursed the little bundle back to health, and Momma started cooking oatmeal and milk for her. She would cook the cereal and then thin it with milk so she could get it through the enlarged nipple of Gela's bottle. Momma also collected all kinds of greens from along the riverbank in the spring, and she would take them, along with any other vegetables she could buy, and cook them until they were very soft. Then she would mash them with a fork and mix them with enough liquid so that they could be fed to Gela through her bottle. Momma spent hours preparing all kinds of food to feed Gela. Once she chewed horse meat until it was fine and then spat it onto a spoon to feed to the baby.

This kind of feeding went on for months. Father was not too hard on us during that time. He was preoccupied with keeping us alive. As long as we did what we were told, everything was all right.

Gela was getting better, but everything else got worse. She was the only joy in my mother's life and our lives. She was so innocent. Her little arms reached out to us as she smiled; she was unaware of the things going on around her.

The Fire

It was sometime in 1948, and I was eight years old. My father had finally been able to get a temporary job with the city. He was helping to pave roads with asphalt. I remember how glad my mother was when Father told her about the job and the income. It was so hard to get work then.

The only bad thing about Father's job was that the asphalt ruined his clothes. To clean them, he bought a large can of gasoline and told Momma to soak all of his clothes in it, which all of the other workers' wives were doing that, and it worked.

Unfortunately, Mother did not know much about gasoline and how dangerous and flammable it was, because she put the open container next to the wood-stove, and the inevitable happened—a spark from the stove ignited the gasoline and the can exploded. Gasoline and flames spread everywhere.

I had been asleep on the sofa behind the kitchen table, and my mother's screams awakened me. I don't know where everyone else was when the can exploded, but Helmut managed to get out of the room with burns only on his hands. Momma grabbed my baby sister, Gela, and rushed her out. Gela received only minor injuries to her forehead.

By the time Momma got the baby to safety, the entire room was in flames. The doorway was the only escape, and it too was engulfed in flames. I was wearing only a little, thin nightgown and had stood up on the sofa. I could see the flames all around me and felt there was no escape. As I stood there, I could feel the fire burning my legs. My nightgown had also caught on fire as had my long braids. I thought I would burn to death, and I covered my face with my hands, but it did no good.

Just before I lost consciousness, I felt someone grab me. When I woke up a few minutes later, I found myself lying on the sofa in the front room of the apartment downstairs. I found out later that our upstairs neighbor had soaked a large blanket with water and used it as a shield to come in and rescue me through the burning doorframe and room.

As I lay there, I suddenly realized that I was totally naked. I guess our neighbor had removed my burning nightgown. It seems strange now, I didn't feel any pain at that moment, but I was so embarrassed to be naked—especially since my neighbor's son, Alex, was standing in the doorway. Alex was about five years older than I, and, fortunately, he had his back to me. I asked him to please get a blanket and cover me up, but he never moved. They told me later that he had been instructed to keep an eye on me while the firemen put out the fire. He was too embarrassed to look at me, so he just stood there by the door making sure I was all right—but not looking!

It wasn't long before a fireman returned to the apartment and put a blanket over me so that he could carry me to the fire truck. It was then I felt the pain. I can remember screaming and screaming, it was so terrible. I thought I was going to die. The pain was so severe, I couldn't stand it. I cried for my mother, and the fireman told me that she was all right and would follow us to the hospital. He also told me that neither Helmut nor Gela had been injured either. That is when I passed out.

I did not wake up until they were putting me on a stretcher in the hospital, and someone removed the blanket. The cold air almost drove me back into unconsciousness, but a kind nurse put a sheet on me and said that a doctor would be with me shortly. My mother suddenly appeared, and I was so glad to see her. I remember asking, "Momma, are you all right?" She looked at me, her face black with smoke. I could see from the way that she was holding her hands that they must have hurt her. I remember saying, "Mommy, I'm hurting so much!"

Just then a nurse walked over with a doctor, and I heard him say, "The hair has to be cut off." I said, "No! No! Not my braids!" but Momma told me that the doctor had to cut my hair off and that most of it was already burnt, and my braids were already gone.

I passed out then; for how long, I don't know. It could have been one day or it could have been five. No one in my family would ever say much about the incident afterward.

I was in the hospital for over six months. Due to the pain and medication, my memories of the first few weeks or months are confusing.

I remember waking up once and finding bandages all over my head, my arms, and my legs. I did find out later that I had first, second- and third-degree burns all over me except for my face and chest.

Another time I remember coming to, to find my mother there with the doctor. I asked my mother if I would look terrible, and she told me that had a very good doctor, that he was one of the best. He was doing some skin grafts on me, but my face was not going to be damaged. I didn't know what skin grafts were, and didn't care, just as long as my face was not going to be scarred or damaged and as long as I didn't feel any pain. I was to find out later that the worst burns were on my legs and that is where the skin grafts were done. I'm not sure exactly how many grafts were done, but I do know that three separate operations were performed.

I can also remember an incident when the doctor removed my bandages and the skin stuck to the bandages. It was so painful, I thought I would scream. Fortunately, the nurse gave me something to make me sleep. The next day, I noticed what appeared to be a huge bubble all over my arms and a part of my legs. I realize now that it was huge blisters. They were filled with water and I didn't notice too much pain until the doctor came and pierced them with a needle to let the water escape. When the blister deflated and the skin touched my body, I was in agony.

As time went on, and I began healing, I was conscious for longer periods of time and more alert and aware of my surroundings. I realized that there were other women in the room with me. One lady in particular was very kind to me. Sometimes, when the nurse was busy, she would feed me. She also read to me at times. The only thing that upset me was when I heard her tell the nurse, "I like that little Helga, but can't the doctor do something about that foul smell? I can't stand being near her." I was hurt, but did not know that burn victims always had a foul smell from the skin rotting. She still helped me, but, after that, I was always careful to pull a sheet over me when she came near me.

As I got better, I realized that I had very few visitors compared to the other patients in my room. My father finally visited me, bringing me some red wine and one raw egg. Germans believe that wine is good for the blood, so even young children are allowed to drink it. Personally, I hated red wine, especially when my father would stir a raw egg into it. It tasted terrible, but he fixed a glass for me and made me drink all of it. He did not stay long, and only came to see me again one more time during my entire stay. I hoped that he would leave the wine at home on that visit, but he brought it with him again.

I don't know where he got the wine or who had told him about the cure. My father had a cure for everything: wine and eggs for the blood; dog grease for boils and sores; beer for pregnancy; peppermint and a camomile for upset stomach; and, of course, cod-liver oil for everything from cough to diarrhea! If I had to cough, I would run outside so he could not hear me! It was a standby for years to come.

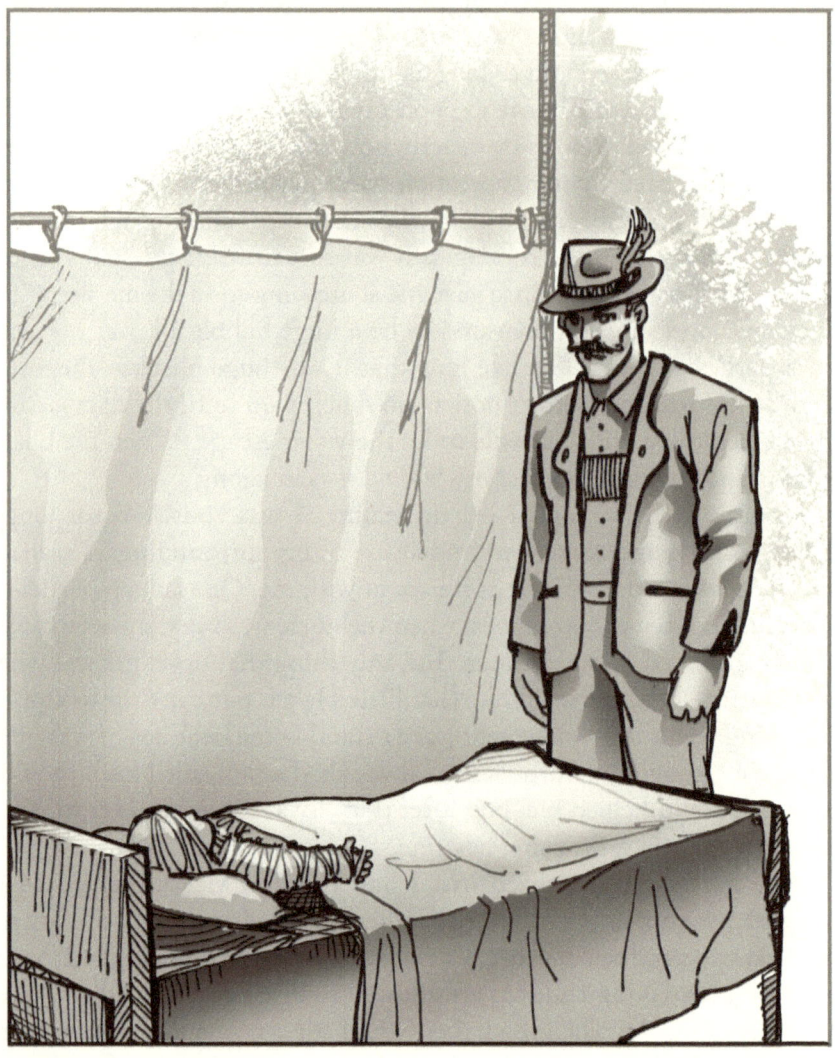

One of the biggest surprises while I was in the hospital was that my grandfather came to see me one day. I could not believe my eyes. I had never seen my grandfather. He and my father had not spoken since my father had run away from home at an early age. When my grandfather walked into the room, I did not recognize him of course. I was astonished when this tall, tall man—he was about six four—told me he was my grandfather. I could not believe it. He looked nothing like my father, who was only five two. The only similarity was that they both had large hands and feet.

Apparently, my grandfather had read in the newspaper about the fire and my burns. He was a nice, friendly, man, and I soon warmed up to him. He told me nice stories about my father and spoke only good of him. Before he left, he gave me five marks and told me to buy something nice with them. I was thrilled! I had never seen so much money in my life. I hid the money under my pillow. When he left, I hoped that I would see him again soon.

The next time my father came to visit, I told him about Grandfather. He was furious and called the nurse in to give her strict orders that my grandfather was not to be allowed near me again. I was heartbroken. Grandfather had been so nice to me. I made an effort to speak up for him and told my father how nice he had been and all of the nice things he had said about Father. Unfortunately, I also told him about the five marks he had given me. My father remained adamant about Grandfather not seeing me again and of course insisted that I give him the money.

My mother's visits were different. She tried to bring me things I liked. She brought my doll to me once, but the nurses would not let me have it, because, with the open wounds, the chances of infection were great. I was not allowed to touch anything except hospital items, which had been sterilized. Momma would read to me, though, and tell me about Helmut and Gela. No matter how bad things were at home, she always had something good to report.

I looked forward to these visits, since I was totally bedridden for several months. The day finally came, though, when the doctor said I could get out of bed. My first trip was to be to the bathroom. I'm not sure how long I had been in the hospital, but, when the nurse came to help me, I could not walk. She called the doctor who said he was afraid of that. He gave her instructions on exercises that would enable me to walk again. It was painful and took several weeks before I could walk normally once more.

As I was getting better, I finally felt my head one day and realized that all I could feel were short whiskers of hair. When I told Momma, she told me how glad she was that my hair was growing back and that, in a few years; I would have long braids again. By the time I got out of the hospital, she had sewn a nice turban for me to cover my head, so that the kids in school would not make fun of me.

I was finally healed and allowed to return home. The fire had completely burned the apartment and destroyed all of our belongings. We had lost everything except for the basket Gela had been sleeping in and the stove in the kitchen. When I got home, my parents had replaced the only bed with a double bed. The entire family now slept in that one bed. The landlord had repaired the apartment as well as he could, but informed us that we had to move within the year.

It may sound funny, but the thing I regret most having been destroyed by the fire was all of the pictures of my mother had of the family. I don't think there were many, especially during the war years, but they are all gone. I have no pictures now of what I looked like as a baby or child. The earliest picture I have of myself now is as a twelve-year-old. It's difficult to remember what I looked like before.

My grandfather never did return to the hospital to see me. When he was there, though, he told me that he had always wanted to visit with his grandchildren, but my father wouldn't let him. When I got home from the hospital, I learned where he lived, and I would visit him secretly. My father's mother had died, and my grandfather had remarried. His new wife was wonderful, as was my grandfather.

As we were getting our lives together again after the fire, the Church was one of our biggest helps. Our wonderful minister again allowed us to find clothes and assisted us in finding furniture and other necessities.

Close Calls

I do believe that I am the luckiest person in the world. I must have nine lives, like a cat. There were so many times that I could have lost my life, but I survived them all!

One time, I got hit by a banana truck. It didn't really hurt me, but the guilty driver supplied us with bananas for a month! Then, of course, there was the sickness and the fire, but that wasn't all. I remember one time we had just gotten back from Colmar and moved into the apartment in Mannheim. My mother had left me with a neighbor woman while she went out for a time. Evidently, the neighbor woman also left me alone while she went shopping. Getting bored of being all alone, I started to play with some buttons on the gas stove. I had never seen a gas stove before. Before I knew it, the entire room was full of gas, and I had no way to escape, because the neighbor woman had locked the door when she left. When I was unable to breathe, I put my mouth up to the front door, which had a small crack under it. I don't know exactly how I got out of the apartment, but I woke up in my own bed. I still wonder how they got into the apartment with me blocking the door.

Another time, I was still very little, and my mother had taken Helmut and me to the marketplace in Mannheim. It was my birthday, and I had ten pfennigs in my hands, which Momma had given me. There was a beautiful statue in the middle of the marketplace surrounded by a deep fountain. The sides of the fountain were very slimy and slippery. I was playing in the water, when, all at once, my ten pfennigs fell into the deep water. Trying to reach the money, I fell into the water too, and there was no way I could get out of the fountain, since the sides were too slippery. I could not swim, and I started to drown. Mother must have been talking to someone, and she did not see what had happened. Helmut, however, having seen the accident, jumped in after me to save me, but he was unable to get a foothold, and he started to drown too. I don't know how Helmut and I got out; I just remember coming to, laying beside the water fountain, as people looked at us, saying, "I guess they're all right now."

Another time, while I was asleep, an electric cord near our bed, attached to the wall for a light, had found its way around my neck. The cord was also wound around the bed. The more I tried to get away from the cord in my sleep, the tighter it wound itself around my neck, choking me. Evidently, Mother woke up and took the cord off my neck. My neck hurt for days afterward. I heard Momma tell Aunt Rosel the next morning that my neck was completely raw from trying to get loose, but I had hardly made a sound.

The worst thing, however, happened one day when Helmut and I were near the castle. The castle had a huge park behind it. It was overgrown after the war. A man came up to Helmut and me and told us he would give us each one mark if we would help him look for his dog, which he said had just run off. He described his dog and told Helmut to go in one direction and me to go in another to give better coverage. We were both glad to oblige. Helmut took off in one direction. The man and I began running in the opposite direction, and he screamed, "There he is!"

Now, I didn't see the dog at all, but I figured that I would get the money if I helped him find the dog. I could sure use the money. I had plans for it already. Momma sure would have been happy with us coming home with two marks between us. I looked for that dog just as hard as I could, never suspecting anything wrong. We were getting to a really dense part of the park when the man said to me, "Why don't we get behind those bushes?" and he pointed to some dense growth. "I'm sure the dog will come by here sooner or later; then we'll catch him."

Still not suspecting anything wrong, I did as he said and went into the underbrush and sat on the ground, just as he told me to. The man sat down beside me. Suddenly, I noticed a briefcase in his hand—I had not seen it before, but all at once I noticed the man slowly opening the briefcase and reaching inside of it. I looked at the briefcase, and then I looked at him. He had the most peculiar look on his face. I really got scared and tried to get up to run away from him, but he grabbed me with one hand as he pulled a silk scarf out of his case with the other hand. I tried to scream, but words would not come out of my mouth!

His hand with the silk scarf went behind my back, the other on my mouth. I knew right then the man meant to do me harm. I knew he had lied and probably never even owned a dog. I started to fight, but he was a large man. I felt this would be the end of me as he tried to put the silk scarf around my neck. Then I heard something. The man heard it too and leg go of me for just a second. I immediately took that opportunity to get away from him and run out from behind the bushes. As I did, I ran smack into Helmut. It was Helmut that we had heard. He had gotten suspicious and came after us. I told him everything as the man ran past us. Helmut started yelling after him and following him as he tried to get out of the park. There was only one exit, and we were hoping that a policeman would come by, but the man got away. We never saw him again.

One really funny incident happened, though. There was a little man who lived in Mannheim, and every time there was a gathering or demonstration in the marketplace, such as the peddlers showing a new kitchen knife or some other gadget, this little man would get behind me or some other little girl and touch her bottom! Well, I sure gave that pervert a nasty look when he did that to me one day! I had seen him around, and I told Helmut about him. We knew it was useless to tell the police, because the little man was a respected retired attorney. It would be his word against ours. One other little girl we knew told us that her father had turned him in, but he was out within an hour.

Well, Helmut and I decided to get even with that little man, and we made a plan. We were not scared of him; he had to be taught a lesson. One day, we actually went looking for him. We found him at a large gathering in the marketplace. The plan we had was for me to get in front of the man in the crowd, and then, if he dared touch me, I was to give Helmut a signal. Helmut then would grab a woman's bottom that was standing beside me and in front of the little man. Helmut would then tell the woman that he had seen the little man grabbing her. In reality, it would be Helmut doing the grabbing. This time the little man would not get away with doing his dirty deed on me!

We knew that man would not be punished if I screamed, but what would happen with a grown woman? We hoped for the best. Helmut had decided that I should find an extra large woman to stand beside to pull off our plot, and finally we found her. There she stood, right next to me, as the little man moved in on me. The crowd was quite large, but Helmut was able to sneak up on the unsuspecting man. Helmut stood right behind him, and, when the man touched my bottom, I gave the signal by lifting my elbow straight up in the air. When Helmut saw this, he reached in front of the little man and really grabbed the bottom of the large woman standing by me!

The woman turned around, indignant and red faced! Helmut told her that he had seen the little man grab her, and I said, "He grabbed me too!" (He really had.)

That woman got so mad, and I still laugh to this day, thinking about what followed. It was hard for the little man to get away in the crowd, which now had gathered around all of us. Everyone looked at the little man as the large woman hit him with her huge handbag several times. Everyone started laughing, and he finally got away, with the woman screaming after him, "You dirty pervert!" I almost felt sorry for the little guy! His reputation and ego must have been pretty shaken and deflated by that time. I'm sure it was quite some time before he ever touched anyone's bottom again!

Helmut

One terrible day, Helmut and I were looking for scrap, but we had not found one thing to sell. I was worried, because I knew we had to go home with money or my father would beat us. We had looked around everywhere, but with no luck. Then Helmut spotted it—an iron supporting beam about twenty feet or more in length. It reached from one wall to the other on the third floor of a shelled house. There was nothing holding the two walls together except that one iron beam.

The only way of getting up to the beam was to climb up on some loose brick. The stairway of the house was gone, probably removed by other scavengers. Helmut started to climb up. "Please don't go," I begged. "You'll be killed." But he would not listen.

I just stood there watching as he climbed to the beam. He finally made it and started to loosen the beam by knocking off the surrounding bricks. He called down to me, "Watch this! I'm going to walk on the beam to the other side of the wall!"

"Please don't!" I begged again.

"Well, how do you expect me to loosen the beam on the other side?"

"Just come down and forget it," I said.

"And get a beating when we get home? No way!" Helmut replied.

With that, he started to balance himself as he walked across the beam. I had never seen him do anything like that in his life. He was on the third floor, and I was so afraid that if he fell he would be killed. It seemed like an eternity, but he finally made it to the other side, and I sighed with relief.

It wasn't long before he had loosened the beam on the other side. "Watch out!" he yelled as he dropped the heavy beam. Then, like a monkey, he climbed back down. Helmut certainly was daring!

Well, there it was. That heavy, large iron beam would bring us a king's ransom in money! We could get enough money for it to last for several days. Father was satisfied if we earned just one mark a day, and Helmut and I had quickly learned, if we earned more than that in a single day, to save the rest for a bad day.

"How much do you think we'll get for it?" I asked Helmut.

"About ten or twenty marks," he replied.

Our next problem was getting the beam to the junkyard. Fortunately, we always took our wagon with us whenever we went scavenging, the same homemade wagon Momma had pulled me in on our walk from Colmar to Mannheim.

It had not been hard for Helmut to push the beam off the wall, but now it was impossible for us to lift it onto the wagon. We had to wait and hope that someone would come by to help us. Finally, we were lucky and two young men came by on bicycles. We stopped them and asked for their help. They were kind enough to give a hand, and, together, we managed to get the beam onto the wagon. The poor wagon almost broke under its heavy load, but we were on our way to the junk dealer. I was so happy!

We were almost there when a policeman suddenly appeared. I had never seen him before; I guess he must have been new on the force. We had never been stopped for scavenging before, but I figured our beam was probably valuable. My heart sank. There we were, almost to the junkyard, and only minutes away from all that money and security from Father and his beatings. I thought of the food it would buy, and I started to cry. Father would probably beat us for getting into trouble.

The policeman made us go with him to the police station, which was also nearby, about a block from the junk dealer. Helmut and I followed the officer, pulling our wagon with the beam on it, behind us. As we pulled in front of the station, the policeman told Helmut and me to come with him. Then, on second thought, he said, "One of you had better pull your wagon to the rear of the station."

I volunteered, and the policeman took Helmut with him into the station. As I pulled the wagon around the corner and toward the back of the station, which was in the direction of the junkyard, I started thinking to myself, "If I go back into the police station, I'll get a whipping. But if I don't go, I'll also get a whipping."

Well, I asked God what to do; he was my only answer. "God," I said, "would you be mad at me if I sold the beam? I'm so hungry. If you think I should not, then please give me a sign, like, make it thunder."

Well, I was too scared to go into the police station, so I took our wagon, beam and all, and left as fast as I could. As I went up a block, I realized that I was almost in front of our junk dealer. I saw him standing outside, waving to me. When I got close, he asked, "My goodness, where did you get that?"

I told him what had happened, and he said that policeman had had no right to stop Helmut and me. Everyone was scavenging." Come in here. I'll take your beam," he said.

"What if the policeman comes here?" I asked.

"Don't worry. I have several more beams just like that," he said and pointed to a pile of steel beams lying in a corner of the junkyard. "No one could ever identify yours or prove that you had brought it in. Besides, you won't get in trouble if you sell the evidence."

I did as he said, and he paid me eighteen marks! I was thrilled! It was a king's ransom, just as I had imagined. *It was worth it after all*, I thought, as I remembered how hard we had worked getting that beam. Helmut could have gotten killed up there on the third floor.

I left for home then, and the junk dealer waved at me as I went out the door. I was scared though, wondering what had happened to Helmut. I was so afraid there would be a policeman waiting for me when I got home. *Well*, I thought, *I'll get a beating one way or the other. At least I have some money for food for several days.* The eighteen marks would buy at least eighteen loaves of bread. That certainly would be worth a beating!

I was prepared not to tell anyone about finding the beam or selling it and was deep in thought when I felt a tug on my wagon, It was Helmut!

"Where is the beam?" he asked.

"I sold it," I said and showed him the money.

"Good girl!" he exclaimed. "Guess what I did? When I got into the station and you didn't follow, I figured you had run off. Well, I was not about to give the policeman my name or address and get us both into trouble, so I told them that it was my dinnertime and I was hungry. They were not about to feed me, so they let me go!"

We both laughed and were sure everything would be all right now. The policeman did not know us, so we figured he could not find us. Father was happy when we got home and gave him some of the money. We hoarded the rest and felt good because we did not have to worry about scavenging for a few days; we would have enough money to give Father. I put the money in my long, black wool stockings. There was to be food for several days if I could help it.

Well, we forgot about the policeman, but he remembered us. For some reason, he seemed to be everywhere we went. It seemed as if he was haunting us! We had to watch out for him constantly which made it difficult to make any money. He never mentioned the incident or the beam, but we knew that should he catch us doing anything wrong, we would not get away. He was not like the other policemen on the force; one of them had stopped Father from beating me one time, and another one lived on our street. They both knew what we were doing, but they also knew it was the only way we could survive.

One day, Helmut and I discovered a house that was being excavated. Those kinds of houses were good to find, because we could always find some kind of scrap in them. The excavating would uncover new places or rooms under the rubble. Helmut told me to wait outside and disappeared in the dark basement of the house. He had barely gotten inside when there came our policeman!

"Where is your brother?" he questioned.

I was afraid to tell him that Helmut was in the house, fearful that he had found something that we were not allowed to have. I just shook my head as if I did not know.

"Aha!" he said, looking at the hole leading into the dark basement. He quickly went after Helmut. I wanted to warn Helmut, but I knew there was no sense in that. I just waited in front of the basement, expecting the worst.

Suddenly, I heard streams of cursing and cussing! It was coming from the policeman, who was coming back out of the basement. He was wiping his uniform, which was wet. He left without saying another word. As I was wondering what had happened, a red-faced Helmut appeared in the opening.

"What happened?" I asked.

When Helmut told me what had happened, we were both in hysterics! It seems that Helmut, upon entering the house, had had to go to the bathroom quite badly. He was in the process of doing just that when someone behind him, in the dark, called, "What are you doing?"

Well, Helmut said he could not stop urinating as he swung to face the voice in the dark, and evidently, as I had seen, he had urinated all over the policeman!

We saw very little of the policeman after that, and no other policeman ever bothered us. Years later, Helmut and I still laughed about that incident!

That is one of the funny incidents that happened while we were scavenging; others were not amusing at all. The worst thing that ever happened to us when we were scavenging was the following incident, which happened much later.

It was sometime in 1948 or 1949, and Mannheim was being rebuilt. Big cranes were being used to excavate the houses, and a lot of new areas were exposed. We looked for everything: iron, paper, rags—whatever we could find. Everything was being recycled.

One afternoon, Helmut and I found a large house that was being excavated. We knew every bombed house in Mannheim, and we knew that house; it must have been a beautiful home once. We had been there before the excavation, but now we figured we should be able to find more scrap. The men had worked that afternoon and exposed the back of the house, which previously had been covered over with rubble.

The workmen had apparently left without checking over the property, because Helmut and I found an opening into a small room. As we entered, we could not see much, since it was so dark. As our eyes got used to the darkness, however, we could see the room was in perfect shape—not a loose brick, nothing disturbed.

Finally, we could see that we were in a little girl's room. The room was completely furnished, and it contained a little girls' bed, which was very prettily made up, and a dresser. On top of the dresser was a dollhouse. It looked as if someone had just been playing with it. There were pretty dolls on the bed.

We could not see any dirt anywhere. In a darker section of the room, I could make out a rocking chair, a child's rocking chair. There was a large doll sitting in the rocker, and it was holding another doll.

I thought it was the prettiest room I had ever seen. It looked as if it had just been fixed up the day before. I had never seen a dollhouse like the one in that room, and I said, "Helmut, let's take the dolly and dollhouse home for Gela."

All of a sudden, Helmut started to cry, "Oh, no! No!" and he pulled me out of the little room.

As Helmut's eyes had gotten used to the dark, he had been able to see that the large doll sitting on the rocking chair was really a little girl. We heard later that she must have died of a gas-leak and just died sitting there, holding her doll. With the house buried, and no air getting into the room, her body must have been preserved.

Thank God, I did not see her face. All that I could tell was she was wearing one of those ruffled hats that children wore then. Her nightgown was too long for me to see her arms and legs. In addition, it was very dark in there, the only light coming from the small opening through which Helmut and I had entered.

I still think about that incident sometimes, and I remember that poor little girl who never lived to grow up, to go to dances, meet a boy, get married, and have children of her own with dolls of their own. Her life was snuffed out before she had ever really lived. I'm only glad that Helmut pulled me out of the room before I had a chance to see her face. It would probably haunt me today. Helmut never told me what she looked like.

When I think about things like that, I wonder who on Earth has the right to do such gruesome things to children. I often made believe that it was just a nightmare, but, as I grew up, I realized I couldn't always pretend that I was dreaming. When I realize that it was real, I get angry, very angry.

All throughout, Helmut was my friend and my closest confidant. He had seen a lot more than me. In years to come, I knew that his past stayed with him, as mine did with me. Helmut never really seemed happy. He was my Rock of Gibraltar, nevertheless. There was nothing he would not do for me. Even when we were far apart at times in our lives, he kept in touch by letter. His letters would be as much as twenty to thirty pages long. He would encourage me and sometimes teach me. He would beg me not to get in trouble and ruin my life. I think through his letters he had more influence on me than any other person in the world except for my mother.

Mother's Agony

I don't know how Momma felt about Strubele; I can only guess. I know that, during 1947 and 1948, my father butchered several other dogs in the basement. It was the only way to stay alive. He was butchering them for other people in our neighborhood, for the neighbors who did not have the heart to butcher their own pets but knew that to survive they would have to do it. Father would give them the cut-up meat wrapped in paper. The neighbors gave him other things in exchange. After I had seen what happened to my poor Strubele, I never ate meat, unless I had seen, with my own eyes, my mother buying it at the store or market.

I will never forget the first time I saw my father butchering a dog. Momma had told me to go and get Father for dinner, and that he was in the basement. I'm sure she didn't know what he was doing; she probably thought he was chopping wood. I went downstairs to get him.

The basement was divided into several stalls, one for each apartment in the building. The stalls were constructed half of wood, half of wire meshed. We kept wood and coal or whatever fuel we had in our stall. When I walked back to our stall, I saw Father with a German shepherd. I recognized the dog, I had seen him before, and the dog belonged to one of our neighbors. Father was just about to hang him up by his front paws when he saw me. He hollered at me, "Get upstairs, and don't come back down here again!"

He didn't have to tell me twice. I never gave him Momma's message about dinner, I just ran upstairs to the bathroom. I did not quite make it and I vomited on the stairway. Since I had not eaten that much, most of my vomiting was water. I sat in the stairway, heaving, my stomach was in an uproar. Momma appeared in the door. "Oh, no," she said, "Helga, You're not getting sick again, are you?"

I just pointed to the basement. She ran by me to see what was so terrible and came back seconds later. Pale and shaken, she went into the kitchen. She returned with a bucket of water and a brush. She did not say a word to me, but started to scrub the staircase, just as hard as she could, cleaning up after me. She looked as if she were trying to scrub away her torment. Father came up a little while later, and we all sat down for dinner. No one spoke. I never told Helmut about the incident or about the dogs, although I think he knew. I didn't tell anyone about anything until years later. I just kept it all inside of me and tried very hard to believe that I was just having bad dreams. I did that quite a lot.

Just before Christmas of 1948, I noticed that my mother seemed to be getting smaller and smaller, and her teeth, her beautiful teeth, were starting to fall out. One morning, I found one of her teeth in the sheets as I helped her to straighten her bed. She acted as if there was nothing to it and told me that she was missing several of them already. She jokingly told me that maybe she would get new ones for Christmas.

Christmas was nice that year, mainly because Momma had tried so hard to make it special. We had a good meal of four large potatoes and 100 grams of Limburger cheese. I can still see Helmut trying to grab the biggest potato and Father beating him to it—almost stabbing Helmut in the hand with his fork! As we finished our portion, Momma told us that she was not hungry and asked if anyone wanted her potato. Not waiting for an answer, she just cut it in half and gave half to Helmut and half to me. I told her I wanted her to eat it, that I had had enough, when Father took the potato from my plate, gave it back to Momma, and made her eat it.

That Christmas Day went by so fast. Momma took Helmut and me to the Catholic Church for mass, while Father stayed home with baby Gela. It seemed so hard for Momma to get around in those days. When we knelt in church, she was unable to get back up. Helmut and I had to lift her. By then, she was not very heavy; I would guess that she weighed about seventy-five pounds. After mass, she had to lean on Helmut and me as we walked home.

We also went to see Uncle Willi and Aunt Rosel that Christmas day. Aunt Rosel had baked a cake, and Helmut and I sat down with them and enjoyed milk and cake. It was a nice visit. Helmut and I loved them both. Uncle Willi also loved Helmut, Gela, and me. His wife, My Aunt Rosel, was the salt of the earth, and she always welcomed Helmut and me into her home. Uncle Willi and Aunt Rosel never had children of their own.

Aunt Rosel was my mother's best friend and confidante. There was nothing Aunt Rosel didn't know about us. Unfortunately, Father and Aunt Rosel had a falling out one day, and Aunt Rosel told Father off; she was like that. No one stepped on her. I know Uncle Willi never laid a hand on her; he always treated her with respect. Unlike Father, Uncle Willi did not believe in hitting a woman or child. Soon, Father also forbade Uncle Willi from entering our house. Uncle Willi still visited us, though; he would come over when Father was at work or standing in line trying to get work.

It was in early March of 1949 that something terrible happened. Things had gotten continually worse for us since everyone else had moved from the apartment and we had to pay the entire rent ourselves. I had turned nine years old, and Helmut had turned eleven. Little Gela was eighteen months old. She was still little, but she seemed to be getting along fine. One day, when Uncle Willi was visiting, my mother told him that she was "really sick."

Uncle Willi begged her to see a doctor. Fortunately, Momma always listened to his advice; she knew he meant well, and she went to the doctor the next day. That night, I heard her tell Father she would have to go to the hospital to have her breasts removed. I didn't understand what was wrong with her.

The decision was made, however, and all the other arrangements were seen to. Gela was to stay with a neighbor, while Helmut and I would stay at home with Father. They told Helmut and I that Momma would be in the hospital for six weeks. I was worried, but Momma told me that if I had any problems, I should go and see Aunt Rosel or Uncle Willi. I wasn't to let Father know of course, since he hated them both. He once said that Uncle Willi was always meddling in our business.

Well, everything was set, and Momma left for the hospital. I was surprised, however, to find her back home again the same day. She said she was not going to the hospital after all. She didn't tell me why, but I was glad that she was home. After I had gone to sleep that night, though, I was awakened by the sound of voices—Mother and Father were talking and I heard Mother telling Father that the doctor had sent her home after he found out she was pregnant again. Father was incensed when he heard that; he had not known she was again expecting.

"I can't understand that! You can't be pregnant!" he said. "Why don't they go on with the operation anyhow?" I couldn't hear what else was said that night, but, over the next few weeks, they were constantly arguing.

One night, Father told her that she better "get rid of that pregnancy." I don't know what her answer was. The next day, she talked to Uncle Willi and told him what was happening.

"Lisa," he said, "You had better not do anything foolish."

"But Willi, I'm afraid of Adam," she answered.

"Go see your doctor and see what he says" was Uncle Willi's advice. I don't know if she went to the doctor or not, but I'll never forget what happened that night.

I saw the way Father looked when he came home and did my best to stay out of his way. Nothing much was said over the meager dinner we had, but, as soon as Father thought Helmut and I were asleep, he told Momma, "Tomorrow, you get rid of that pregnancy or I'll get rid of it."

"No, Adam, please, I can't get rid of the baby. We'll be able to feed it somehow," I heard her say.

"What! Like Gela?" he hollered. "You can't even nurse her; you know your milk is not good. Look what happened to Gela! She almost died." Momma just cried. Finally, Father said, one last time, "Tomorrow, while I'm gone, you get rid of it—or I will." Then he went to sleep.

I was awake most of the night and could hear Momma crying all through the night. I wanted so badly to go to her and hug and comfort her, but I did not move because I knew Father would beat me if he had any idea that I had heard them talking. I didn't know or understand about abortions then, and I just lay there wondering about what was going to happen the next day and remembering how Father had jumped on Mother's stomach when she was expecting Gela. Momma was probably thinking about that too. I had to stuff the corner of my pillow in my mouth to keep from crying out loud and waking Father.

The next day was March 16, 1949—a day I will remember until I die.

Morning had finally come, and Father had left for work. It was about 6:00 A.M., and Helmut was still asleep. I was awake and noticed that Momma was still in bed, which was unusual. When she noticed that I was awake, she asked me to do an errand for her. I said I would, and she wrote a note and put it into an envelope, along with some money. As she sealed the envelope, she told me where to take it; it was not far.

I left as soon as I got dressed and hurried to the address Momma had given me. It was an apartment house. I knocked the door and waited. Soon, a man answered the door. He was still in his pajamas. A woman came up behind him. When he asked what I wanted, I gave him the envelope. He opened it, read the note, and looked at the woman, who then disappeared into the apartment. The man and I remained standing outside until finally the woman yelled, "Make her come in and close the door!"

We went inside the apartment then, and stood by the door. In a few minutes, the woman reappeared with a package in her hands. She gave it to me and told me to take it to my mother. I took the package and left, but not before the woman made sure that no one was looking and that I wouldn't be seen as I left. I thought she was acting rather strangely.

Momma was waiting for me when I got back. She didn't open the package, but told me to put it on the kitchen table;. I was curious about it, but she didn't say a word. I found out years later that it was an instrument used for abortions.

When I got back, I found that Helmut had gone on to school without me. He usually walked with me, but that morning, Momma had sent him on alone. As I gathered my things to leave, she called me back into the bedroom and told me to sit down, on the bed. She said she wanted to tell me something very important.

I still remember the look on her face as she talked to me; it was as if she was about to tell me the most important thing in her life. As she talked, I could sense the urgency of her words and could feel the importance she placed on them. "Helga," she said, "I won't always be here. If something should happen to me, would you please take care of your little sister, Gela?"

I tried to tell her that nothing would happen to her and please, not to talk like that, but she continued.

"Please, Helga, please promise me that you will take care of Gela. You are the only one I can trust." Tears started running down her face then, and the urgency in her voice made me hug her and say, "I promise, Momma. I promise I will always take care of Gela." She kissed me good-bye then and watched me as I left the room.

That morning in school all I could think about was my mother and how she had looked when I left. About eleven o'clock, I felt as if Momma was calling out for me, that she needed me. I don't know what it was, or why I felt that way, but I ran out of my classroom, disregarding everything my teacher said, and ran all of the way home, almost flying up to the second floor. When I tried to get in the kitchen door, I found the door locked. "Momma, Momma! Please open the door!" I cried.

When the door did not open, I pressed my ear close and listened. I thought I heard her breathing; I felt her presence. There was light coming from under the door, so I knew that she was in the kitchen. I thought I heard her call out to me.

When Momma didn't open the door, I got scared and confused. I didn't know what to do. Finally, I ran to Helmut's school, hoping he would have a key, but he did not. Helmut sensed the urgency and terror in my face and voice and ran back home with me, leaving his school too. It was between eleven-thirty and twelve then.

Helmut could not get the door open either. "We have to get in there," I screamed, "before it's too late!"

Helmut just looked at me. I don't know if it was the tone in my voice or what, but he didn't say a word as he quickly ran down the steps and across the street, where there was a building under construction. He grabbed a piece of lumber and came rushing back; he couldn't have been gone more than a few minutes.

"Stand back!" he yelled and knocked in a part of the door with the piece of lumber. He then reached inside, unlocked the door, and swung it open. We rushed in, and I saw the most terrible sight I had ever seen.

My mother was lying on the couch. She was fully dressed. Her eyes were staring at the ceiling. My baby sister Gela was clutched to her chest; both looked blue and lifeless. On the floor was a pan of blood. Next to the pan were several sheets and pillow cases, they were all soaked with blood.

I just stood there.

Suddenly the man from upstairs, the same man who had saved me from the fire, pushed past Helmut and me. He was home for his lunch and had come running down when he heard us breaking the door. We watched as he pried Gela out of Momma's arms. It seemed hard for him to do; Momma was holding her that tightly. As soon as Gela was freed, she gasped for breath, and the color came back into her face.

"Thank God. We got to her just in time," our neighbor said and handed Gela to his wife, who had followed him into our apartment. She took Gela and went back to her apartment upstairs.

Our neighbor, meanwhile, had gone back to Momma. He was feeling her pulse and listening to her chest. My eyes remained on him every second as he worked over her. I felt terror in my heart when I saw him close her eyes. I tried to get closer to Momma, but Helmut got in front of me and pushed me out the kitchen door.

Everything happened so fast, and suddenly there were all kinds of people in front of our apartment. An ambulance appeared with two men and a doctor. As they passed by me with a stretcher, I tried to get back into the kitchen, but Helmut and a neighbor grabbed me and held me back.

"Let me back in!" I cried, "I want to kiss Momma goodbye! Please, I've got to kiss Momma goodbye!"

The doctor came back out after a while and asked about Gela. Someone told him where she was, and he went upstairs to check on her. I watched for him to come back down, just standing there, hoping this was all a dream.

When the doctor finally returned to our apartment, a neighbor asked him if the "little Braun girl was all right" and he said that she would be fine. The neighbor then asked him how Frau Braun was, and the doctor just shook his head.

The doctor never spoke to Helmut and me, but, as the men from the ambulance carried Momma past Helmut and me, I saw the doctor looking at the neighbors and again shake his head. When Momma was carried out, I could see that she was totally covered with a white sheet.

"No! No! Momma, you can't leave me!" I screamed and tried to throw myself on the stretcher. One of the neighbors grabbed me and pulled me back as I asked, "Doctor, you will take good care of her?"

The neighbor held onto me until the ambulance left. After that, I tried to go back into the kitchen to pray in our praying corner, but the apartment was a mass of confusion. The police had arrived, and there were already a few of the neighbor ladies cleaning up. They told me that it was all right if I wanted to go into the bedroom and lie down.

I rushed past them into the bedroom. When I got there, I found Momma's sweater lying on a chair. I took the sweater and put it around me; it felt as if it had a part of her still in it. Then I crawled into a corner of the bedroom and just sat there—I don't know for how long.

The bedroom door was open, and I could hear everything going on out in the kitchen. It was hectic, and there was all kinds of commotion. Father was still at work. I heard the policeman telling someone there would be an investigation. One of the neighbors told the policeman that had it not been for Frau Braun's children (meaning Helmut and me), the little girl, Gela, would be dead too. She couldn't understand how we had gotten out of school so early. I also heard her tell the policeman that the doctor had told her husband that my mother had died between eleven and eleven-thirty that morning—the same time I felt her calling out to me.

I just sat there listening. I still didn't believe it was happening. Finally, another woman came into the kitchen. She was a mean, spiteful person, and I had never liked her. I heard her say, "I think Frau Braun tried to take that little girl, Gela, with her." Had I not been so terribly frightened, I would have run out there and told that terrible woman that was not true! It was an accident, I was sure Momma did not want to take Gela with her. She had made me promise to take care of her, just that morning! Momma wanted Gela to live. I know that Momma loved Gela and wanted only good for her! I wanted to tell that terrible lady these things, but I couldn't;

I just sat in the corner with Momma's sweater held tightly around my shoulders.

Finally, I heard Father talking to someone in the kitchen. I had not heard or seen him come into the apartment, but still I sat in the corner. When I realized that everyone had gone, I went out into the kitchen just in time to see Father sit down and put his head on the kitchen table. Everyone was gone, even Helmut. Father sat there, alone, his shoulders shaking. I guessed he was crying. I walked over to him, I knew how he felt. I put my arm around his shoulders and said, "Papa"—I seldom called him Papa—"Papa, I love you." Father had stiffened at my touch, and just as I was about to tell him that he still had Helmut, Gela, and me, he looked at me, and with a wild look on his face said, "Don't you ever tell me you love me. It's all your fault! If it hadn't been for you children, she would be here today!"

I started to back away from him as he screamed at me, but not soon enough. He jumped up from his chair and, with his fist, hit me so hard in the pit of my stomach that I was lifted off the floor. I hit the wall across the room and lay on the floor, not making a sound, just trying to catch my breath. Father didn't look at me again, but just got up and left the apartment.

I don't know which had hurt me worse, his words or the pain in my stomach. I just lay there on the floor unable to get up. Finally, I managed to crawl over to the cross on the wall, Momma's cross, and prayed to God. I begged him to send Momma back to me, or to come and get me—I was so scared. I also told him I was sorry about Momma.

Helmut finally came into the kitchen. I don't know where he had been. Helmut always ran off somewhere when there was something going on.

He sat beside me and tried to comfort me as I started to vomit blood. He hurried and cleaned it up for me.

Father returned after a while and acted as if nothing had happened. My stomach was still hurting badly, but I did not let Father know. I still could not get up, so I just pulled Momma's sweater tighter around me and fell asleep sitting under the cross in the kitchen. The next morning, when I woke up, I was in my own bed. I guess Father had put me there.

The next day, May 17, 1949, Father took me aside and told me that the police would be there soon. He told me exactly what to say when they questioned me. I was not to tell them anything that I might have heard or anything that I might have seen. Under no circumstances was I to tell them about the package or the people who had given it to me.

Shortly afterward, two policemen arrived. As one of them questioned me, I did exactly as Father had said: I told them nothing. I just sat there with Momma's sweater around me, holding the sleeve to my face. Finally, the other policeman told the officer questioning me that it was useless, to just let me go. They then questioned Helmut, who answered as truthfully as he could, which was fairly easy, because Helmut had not seen anything and he didn't know where I had gone that morning or about the package.

As I was to find out years later, my mother had bled to death trying to abort her pregnancy, as Father had told her to do. She had used the instrument in the package, the one I had gotten that morning. I felt so evil.

After the policemen left, I could not get Father's words out of my mind: "It's all your fault!" I could hear them over and over again. I felt so helpless. I believed him; it was my fault. If Momma hadn't had me, none of this would have happened. I felt so helpless. I went into the bedroom, opened the window, crawled out on the ledge, and jumped.

To my disappointment then, I landed on the roof of the bicycle building, which was right under our bedroom window. It broke my fall. I had forgotten about the small building on the first floor. I should have jumped out of the kitchen window, where I would have fallen straight down to the ground, two floors below, but I was confused and jumped from the wrong window. In years to come, I believed it was meant to be like that. I think God had other plans for me.

Helmut had seen me jump, and he was outside. He ran over to see if I was all right. I was; I didn't even have a scratch on me, but I was in a daze. Helmut started to talk to me then. "Helga," he said, "please don't do that anymore."

Tears were streaming down his face and he held my head between his hands and made me look at him. "Don't leave me all alone. I could not stand it if you died too."

His words got through to me, and I started remembering my promise to Momma, that I would take care of Gela. I promised myself that I would never let Momma down again.

That night, Uncle Willi appeared outside in the street in front of our apartment. He was stricken with grief and had obviously been drinking, which was not like Uncle Willi, I had never seen him drink before. He just kept staggering back and forth but did not come up. I heard him scream: "Adam! You killed her! You killed Lisa! You come out here!"

Uncle Willi kept repeating this and the neighbors started to gather outside with him. Finally, Father walked over to the kitchen window and called out, "Go home, Willi! You're drunk!"

My heart went out to Uncle Willi. I knew just how he felt. I had lost my mother, and he had lost his only sister. I wanted so badly to go out and talk to him, but I knew that Father would beat me if I did. Instead, I went into our bedroom and looked out the window, where Father could not see me. I waved to Uncle Willi. When he finally noticed me, he looked straight at me. I could see the love he had for me in his eyes. He looked so much like my mother, with blond hair and deep-blue eyes. I think he started to cry; then he left without saying another word. As he walked away, he pulled his handkerchief from his pocket.

Mother's funeral was the next day. I was not allowed to go, and actually, I didn't really want to go, since Father had told me that it was my fault she had died. Father's words had cut into my heart. The burden was almost too hard for me to carry. The pain in my stomach had gotten better—or maybe I just didn't notice it anymore, because the pain in my heart was so much worse.

That night in my prayers, I told Momma I was sorry for what I had done. I didn't know exactly what I had done, but I promised Momma that I would keep my word and take good care of Gela.

My mother was thirty-seven years old when she died.

Uncle Willi and Aunt Rosel

The next day, May 18, 1949, I stayed out of Father's way as best I could. So did Helmut. Gela was still with the neighbor. Nothing was normal, and I felt as if I were living a nightmare. I kept seeing Momma lying on the couch, her eyes still open. Except for her color, she had almost looked peaceful.

I kept seeing Gela in her arms and remembering how difficult it had been for our neighbor to take her away from Momma. I could still hear the comment that awful lady had made and I wonder if she could be right: did Momma really want to take her baby, Gela, with her? Was she afraid to leave Gela with Father? My thoughts were hurting me as much as Momma's death itself. If I only knew what had gone on in her mind before she died. I thought about everything over and over until my head was hurting. I remembered how Momma had been that morning; it was as if she knew what was going to happen. I was having that same terrible feeling.

Helmut finally put a stop to my self-persecution when he told me that Uncle Willi had been seen in a nearby bar the night before, getting drunk. He kept telling everyone that he was going to kill our father, and it was Father's fault that Momma was dead. He was heard repeatedly saying, "He killed Lisa. He killed Lisa." He told anyone who would listen what a terrible life his sister, Lisa, had had with my father. He told how Father had beaten her for years, making her life miserable, so miserable that she had finally killed herself and her unborn baby. She would be here today if it were not for Adam. "I'm going to kill him for what he did to Lisa," he had vowed.

When Helmut told me that, I went over to see Aunt Rosel to tell her what Uncle Willi was saying. Uncle Willi was at work, and Aunt Rosel didn't really listen to me. She just sat at the table and told me, "Your father is crazy. He is out of his rotten mind. Look how he destroyed your mother! He must think he is God, telling her what to do, and from what I hear, he is getting away with it! The police didn't even arrest him. That animal should be behind bars!"

Aunt Rosel was so distraught and upset over Momma's death, she couldn't listen to me. I remember how close she had been to Momma, how Momma had confided in Aunt Rosel. She knew more about Momma than anyone else.

When I started to tremble and cry, Aunt Rosel finally came to her senses and stopped talking in the middle of what she was saying. She looked at me and said, "Helga, poor Helga. Don't cry. It's not your fault. You didn't do anything wrong."

She muttered something to herself as she gave me a handkerchief to dry my eyes. She didn't say anything about Father after that; she just comforted me. I was hoping that she could have me come and live with her and Uncle Willi, but I knew that was impossible. Father hated her as much as he hated Uncle Willi.

It felt good, though, and made me feel better to know that Aunt Rosel did not blame me for my mother's death. Although deep inside I kept thinking that Father had been right, that if it had not been for us children, my mother would still be alive. I stayed with Aunt Rosel for a while longer and then had to go home.

That night, as it was getting dark, Father, Helmut, and I sat down to eat. A neighbor had brought us some food. None of us could eat, so finally Father put the food into one of our own dishes, washed the neighbor's pot, and told Helmut to return it. After Helmut left, Father sat back down at the table and dropped his head to his arms. He was doing that a lot. I sat on the chair to his left.

Father's back was to the door, which Helmut had left open. For some reason I looked up, and there stood Uncle Willi, a crazy look in his eyes and a pocket knife in his hand, ready to stab Father. When I saw him, I jumped up to stop him. Just as I moved, Uncle Willi plunged the knife toward Father's back. However, I had managed to put my hand in front of Father's back, and Uncle Willi's knife went through my left hand. Uncle Willi stopped and regained his senses as soon as he saw what he had done: my hand was bleeding, with the blade straight through the palm, extruding on the other side.

He immediately pulled the knife from my palm, and I was surprised that I felt no pain. Uncle Willi then pulled out a handkerchief and wrapped it around my hand, saying, "Helga'le, Helga'le . . . ." As he knelt beside me, his words stuck in his throat as our large fire poker came crashing down on his head. Father had hit him with it, and he toppled over like a fallen tree. I screamed as Father tried to hit him again, just as Helmut came through the door. Father stopped and lowered the fire poker, but kept it in his hands.

There was blood seeping from Uncle Willi's skull—not as much as from my hand, but I could see a deep hole in his head. We all just stood there and stared at Uncle Willi. Finally, he started to move. He pulled himself up and staggered out of the apartment. I watched him through the window as he left.

I never saw my beloved Uncle Willi again. Apparently, he staggered home and Aunt Rosel took him to the hospital, where he became unconscious and unable to speak.

I knew in my heart that Uncle Willi had not meant to hurt me. I could smell the alcohol on his breath and knew he had been drunk. Again there was to be an investigation.

The next morning, we were all called to the police station. Father had again prompted me with what to say and what not to say, just as he had done a few days earlier regarding Momma's death. I was not to tell the police that my beloved Uncle Willi was kneeling beside me bandaging my hand as Father hit him. I was to tell the police only that Uncle Willi was about to stab Father and had accidentally stabbed me, when Father hit him.

When the police questioned me, I did not answer. The events of the past few days finally took their toll, and I went into shock. I did not talk again for days.

The police also questioned Helmut, but he was of no help, since he had not entered the room until everything was over and Uncle Willi was lying on the floor. I don't remember what happened after that, but my Father was not arrested this time either.

The assault on me and Uncle Willi also had their effect on Aunt Rosel. She had a breakdown and was placed in a mental hospital. She was released a year later, but she was never the same. As time passed, she was in and out of mental hospitals for the rest of her life. She was finally institutionalized for good.

It was exactly three months after Momma's death that we received word that Uncle Willi had died of his injuries. He was thirty-nine years old.

School

How I ever made it through school after my mother's death is a puzzle to me. I was scared of school, scared of the teachers; they were allowed to use physical force to discipline us. Since I was from a poor family, it had always been hard for me to make friends. I noticed from the beginning that the other children would judge you by the way you dressed and who your family was. As rough as times had been for all of us in Mannheim, my family seemed to have been hit the hardest.

When Momma was alive, I hadn't noticed these things as much. Momma had known how to make do even in the worst of times, but after her death, things got horrible. I had never realized just how much she had done until one of my teachers, my sewing teacher, started to be especially nasty to me. It seemed it was only days after Momma's death when she started picking on me and ridiculing me by saying things like "Helga, do you ever brush your teeth?" or "Helga, do you ever wash? Just look at your neck." It wouldn't have been so bad if only she had taken me outside to talk to me, but instead she would say these things and ridicule me in front of the rest of the class, who would all laugh and snicker. One day she said, "Helga, your knitting is the worst in this entire class," and with that she took the sock I had been knitting and pulled it apart. Hours of work lay there in a puddle of wool on the floor, getting dirty.

Another time, she asked, "You know, you are going to fail this class, don't you?" She was a woman of her word, and I failed that term. I think she thought of me as her private pest. Because of her, I began to dread knitting class so much that I would practically get sick just before her class. None of the other children bothered with me. I guess they were all scared of her.

Finally, things started to settle down, and just when I thought she could not hurt me anymore, she really humiliated me. One morning, she came over to my desk and, holding two pencils in her hand, she started to part my hair with great disdain and asked, "Helga, when was the last time you were deloused?"

I remembered the last time Father had deloused me; it was just before Mother had died. Father had poured a half-gallon of petrol over my head and almost set me on fire with his ever-present cigarette. I hated getting deloused. The petrol would burn my skin, and I was not allowed to wash my hair for a day afterward; it was terribly messy.

I'm sure I had lice, but I did not think it was fair for her to pick on me alone, so I told her, "I'll bet the other kids have lice too."

The teacher was quite surprised at my response. She was not used to anyone speaking up for himself in her class. She called me to the front of the class and made me stick my hand out. She hit me with her stick as she told me that would teach me to speak out when I was not asked to. Because of her hitting my hands, I was unable to do my knitting that day, and, of course, she gave me a bad mark for not doing my work.

That night, before going to bed, I knelt in front of Momma's cross, the one she had kept in the kitchen. It had been a little while since I had talked to God, but I talked to him then. I told him of all of my trouble and how I missed my mother and how I had no one to talk to, not even in school. I asked him if he could come and get Helmut, Gela, and me so we could all be together again with Momma. That night, I washed myself really well. I also gave Gela a sponge bath. Then I went to bed, folded my hands, and waited. Nothing happened.

Gela woke me up bright and early the next day. I was disappointed that God had not come to get me and thought maybe it was because of the lice. That evening, I had father delouse me. After everyone had gone to sleep, I got up and went over to the cross and whispered, "God, are you listening? I brushed my teeth, I washed really carefully, and I even got deloused. We are all ready now. Please come and get us." I went back to bed, folded my hands, and waited again.

I was heartbroken the next morning when I woke up and found we were all still alive and well. After that second night, I gave up trying to join Mother in heaven. I guessed that God had other plans for me.

One morning, however, only days after the incident with the sewing teacher, we were informed that we were getting a new sewing teacher. Our present teacher, we were told, had left our school to pursue a career elsewhere. Rumor had it that she had been fired. When I heard that, I realized that God had been listening to me after all. Our new sewing teacher was extremely nice, and she never picked on me or singled me out for abuse and ridicule. As a matter of fact, when she found out that my mother had just died, she went out of her way to be nice to me. When some of the other children noticed how nice the teacher was being to me, they too started to be nicer. It was my new sewing teacher also who noticed the bruises on my face one day and reported it to the principal. My father was called in for a meeting, and, while I don't know exactly what happened, Father did stop beating me for a short while.

I do remember some good times at school before Momma died. One Christmas, just before the fire, we had a play at school. Because of my long blond hair, I was chosen to be an angel. Momma made my costume out of an old, worn sheet. I was so proud; Momma had brushed my hair until it shone, and she let it fall all around my shoulders. She had also made a halo for me, out of foil. The day of the play, nearly all of the parents were there except mine. Momma was sick at home, and Father stayed home with her. I was disappointed, but when everyone told me what a nice angel I made, I was happy.

Another nice time was when all of the children got a small plant to raise. Momma saved eggshells and soaked them in water to make fertilizer. I had to carry the plant from one window to the other because there was very little sun hitting our apartment, and I wanted to catch every ray of sun. I won third prize that year over the whole school. The first three prizes were large pots filled with flowers called Alpenveilchen.

And then, of course, there was my homeroom teacher, Herr Lehrer Ahr. He really liked my short stories about class trips that we had taken and plays we had seen. Looking back now, I realize it is because of him I'm writing my book. He believed in me then, and, although he died a long time ago, he still gives me courage today.

The Orphan

From the time she was twelve years old until she was twenty-one, my mother lived in an orphanage. She used to tell me a lot of stories about the orphanage, some quite funny, some not. What I remember most is a haunting song my mother used to sing about a seven-year-old orphan girl.

In the song, the little orphan girl would go to her mother's grave and dig a small hole with her fingers so that her mother could hear her tell about her life with her new stepmother.

I can't remember all of the verses, but the few I do remember go like this:

Und Kämmt sie mir mein Haar,
dann ziegt sie mich sogar.
Aber du liebst Mütterlein du, ja du,
band'st schöne Schleifen dazu.

Und scshmiert sie mir mein Brot,
Da wünscht sie mir den Tod.
Aber du liebst Mütterlein du, ja du,
gabst Butter and Kase dazu.

Und legt sie mich zur Ruhe,
schlagt sie die Türe zu.
Aber Du liebst Mütterlein du, ja du,
Du wünchest mir gute Ruhe.

It is difficult for me to translate this song into English, but it goes something like this:

And when she combs my hair,
she pulls so hard it hurts.
But you, dear Mother, oh you, oh you,
braided in beautiful ribbons too.

And when she gives me bread,
she wishes I were dead.
But you, dear Mother, oh you, oh you,
gave me butter and cheese too.

And when she puts me to bed,
she slams the door instead.
But you, dear Mother, oh you, oh you,
you wished me a good-night, too.

After my mother died, I would go to her grave and, remembering the song, I would talk to her by digging a little hole, just like the orphan in the song—especially after Frau Katuck came to live with us.

Frau Katuck

Frau Katuck was a lady my father had picked up somewhere only a few days after my mother died. I was surprised and dismayed to find her in my father's bed one morning. She was very thin and wiry, practically skin and bones, with short-cropped black hair and very pale skin. She was just the opposite of my mother, who was a very beautiful woman.

Frau Katuck never physically hurt me, but her crude talk, which was coarse and rough like a sailor's, hurt me more than any beating ever could. From the very beginning, she made it a special point to tell all of us about her two small sons, whom she had lost in the war. At first we felt so sorry for her, but, as time went on, we came to hate her for her constant comparison of them to us. Her boys were angels, but we were the scum of the earth—worse yet, "maggots." Because of her and her comments, I would always walk with my head down, so people could not see how ugly I was. She made it quite clear that I could never compare to her towheaded angels.

One example of her cruelty, which I know is funny now, but wasn't at the time, was her telling me that if she took "the crust off my knees, and the cheese from my toes, she would have herself a sandwich." I was only nine years old then and didn't know how to keep myself clean—I've always wondered why she didn't teach me.

I can also still remember my teacher getting mad at me in school for not looking up when he was talking one day. At that time, Herr Lehrer Ahr was the most wonderful person in my life, but, because of my stepmother's constant abuse, I felt I could not hold my head up and have him look at ugly, maggot-faced me. Because of it, he made me stand in the corner. The other kids made fun of me, of course, but that was okay; at least they could not see my ugliness.

Somehow my brother, Helmut, found out about the incident at school and asked me about it. I told him how I didn't want anyone to look at me. He just looked at me and said, "I don't think you look like a maggot. Frau Katuck lied to you." I told him he was just being kind, and he said, "If you don't believe me, look in the mirror."

I was nine years old, and I had never looked in a mirror! I had always seen my father shave with it, but it hung up high, over the sink, and was of no interest to me.

"Go look," Helmut said, and he took me into the front room, got a footstool, and made me look into the mirror for the first time in my life.

When I looked into the mirror, I got one of the biggest shocks of my life—what I saw was one of Frau Katuck's towheaded boys, just as she had described him. I didn't believe it was me, and I got really mad at Helmut for tricking me like that. He said, "No, no, it really is you. Get up there and look again. It's really you. Do something; stick out your tongue—you'll see that it's you."

I did as he said, and I finally believed that it was my reflection I saw in the mirror. But I was shocked. I looked just as Frau Katuck had described her boys. My hair was just growing back from the fire and it was kind of pixie looking and not neat at all, but it was golden just like my real mother's. My face looked just fine, nothing at all as Frau Katuck had said. I was happy. (Unfortunately, I still hold my head down to this day, but now I guess it's just a habit!)

The next time Frau Katuck called me bad names I just looked at her and asked, "Have you looked in Father's mirror? I have." She never said another word about my looks.

In retrospect, I don't think that Frau Katuck was as bad as we had thought. I think I reminded her of her sons, and she must have wondered why I had survived, while her sons were lost, probably dead.

At some point, she caught infectious tuberculosis, and the health department made her move out of our house. I saw her now and then as I got older. I learned that she died in 1972; her neighbors told me she often remembered me in kind words.

Of course, Frau Katuck's leaving made things worse than ever in some ways. We were all checked for TB and were found to be healthy. Now, however, there was no one at all to take care of us except Father, and he did not bother about us at all.

Mother had always taken care of everything. Frau Katuck had taken care of the laundry, cooking, and cleaning. She never took care of Helmut and me personally. No one taught me to take care of myself, not even Momma; she had always given me baths herself. Momma had taught me how to cook and bake, but personal hygiene was not included.

The Orphanage

Frau Katuck's departure was the best thing that had happened to us, we thought. Helmut and I jumped up and down with joy the day she left, suitcase and all. Little did we know that the welfare agency had other plans for us and that the freedom that we were enjoying would last only two or three weeks. We didn't know who did it or why, but either a neighbor or Frau Katuck had reported that we were neglected. The German government was always strict about unattended children.

At the time, Helmut was eleven-and-a-half years old, Gela was two, and I was nine-and-a-half. Personally, I thought we got along fine. Each morning, I fixed breakfast for everyone and then took Gela to a neighbor lady before going to school. I had learned quite a lot about cooking from my mother. I could cook a bean soup and boil potatoes and fix all kinds of other things for dinner, which had to be done before Father got home. I even learned from Frau Katuck, who taught me how to clean the house. I did the laundry and even ironed clothes.

I thought everything was fine, even though I never took a bath or gave Gela one for that matter. Why should I take a bath, I thought, I always hated washing, especially with icy cold water, and now no one made me. Oh, I was in my glory! I loved taking care of Gela. I dressed her, fed her oatmeal, sang to her, and tucked her in her bed each night with a prayer. It was the same one Momma had taught me:

> *Ich bin klein*
> *mein Herz ist rein*
> *darf niemand drin leben*
> *als Jesus allein. Amen.*

which means:

> I am little, my heart is pure
> only Jesus can live in it. Amen.

One day, totally unexpectedly, it happened. A social worker came and took Helmut and me from school and got Gela from her sitter and took us straight to the orphanage. I was crying because I was afraid we were going to be separated, but the social worker assured me that we were all going to the same Catholic orphanage in Schwetzingen. When she said that, I stopped crying and went quietly with her. What she neglected to tell me, however, was that I would not be able to see Helmut and Gela as long as we were there. It was not because the orphanage was cruel, but the orphanage was divided into three separate wings: one for boys, one for girls, and a third wing for infants and small children up to the age of three. The play yard was also separated by a fence.

The social worker dropped me off and left. I was fine until I found out about the separate wings, and then I went to pieces. I begged and begged the Catholic nuns to let me see my brother and sister, but they said there were rules and I could not. I had no idea what was going to happen me or to them and I was so scared. Momma had told me some terrible stories about the orphanage in which she had grown up: not enough food to eat, beatings, being locked in the basement with a demented groundskeeper to watch her. All sorts of terrible things went through my mind.

I remembered one particular story Momma had told me about her stay in the orphanage. Apparently, it had been a terrible place. The children were abused and not given enough food. All of the children had to work on local farms to earn money or food—all of which was turned in to the orphanage. Sometimes, rather than working, the children had to go along and beg the farmers for food. Sometimes, the farmers or their wives would take pity on the children and give them sausage or meat, but the children never got to eat any of it. They were given only starchy foods—bread and potatoes—but never meat.

The older my mother got, the angrier she got that she could not eat any of the meat given to her. Finally, one day when a farmer gave her a sausage, she tied it around her waist under her clothes and sneaked it into her room. She and the other girls giggled all of the way home from the farm, anticipating a delicious sausage sandwich. It was a smoked sausage, so cooking was not a problem. Late that night, my mother crept downstairs to the kitchen to get some freshly baked bread and a knife to cut the sausage. There were about twelve girls waiting upstairs for the long-awaited sandwich, all in their teens like Momma. Everything went along fine. Momma had a loaf of bread and the knife and was climbing back up the stairs. She was almost to the third floor when the demented caretaker appeared out of nowhere. He yelled at her, demanding to know what she was doing. He was standing right above her, on the third floor.

Momma was terrified. She told me that she panicked and tried to get away from him as fast as possible. She put her leg over the banister to slide down, but with the large loaf of bread and knife in her hand, she lost her grip and fell, over the side of the banister, to the floor, three stories below. When she landed, she hit the floor with her right foot. Momma said she remembered hitting the floor and then nothing else until she woke up in the hospital. The fall crippled her for life; her right leg was shoved into her hip, making her right leg two inches shorter than her left leg.

Momma had hopes of becoming a ballet dancer when she got out of the orphanage. She had training for eight years before her parents died. On occasion, she had danced for the orphanage to raise money. But there she was, fourteen years old and crippled. After the fall, Momma put her efforts into learning how to sew and cook. She later became a cook for the famous "Liedertal" restaurant. Momma stayed in the orphanage until she was twenty-one years of age. She married my father when she was twenty-nine years old. Even though she had been beautiful, with blonde hair, blue eyes, and a beautiful smile with teeth like pearls, her affliction made her feel ashamed of herself. She told me once that before the accident, all the boys on the farms would watch her, but afterward, it was as if she had some terrible contagious disease, and they all stayed away from her. People were so cruel in those days, especially with Hitler wanting only "perfect" people.

I began to tremble as I remembered all of those terrible things that happened to my mother. When one of the nuns asked, "Helga, are you hungry?" I was stunned. I was hungry, but no one had ever asked me that before. I told her that I was and she left.

The sisters there were different from anyone I had ever known. I was surprised to find out that they knew all about me—my name, everything—and they were smiling at me. I was shown to a nice room containing four beds. There was also a sort of partition toward the back of the room, the type of curtain used for privacy, but I didn't pay much attention to it. I just stood there and looked around me.

In just a few minutes, a Sister came in and gave me the orphanage outfit, a lovely white blouse and a gray jumper with an apron. Another Sister came in and gave me a large glass of milk and a slice of bread spread with butter. My eyes really popped out at all of these wonderful things happening to me! I sat down and ate, still too surprised to say much of anything.

When I had finished eating, one of the Sisters told me that I was to take a bath. I was not too happy about that, but when she took me by the hand and led me into the bathroom, I was pleasantly surprised. There was warm water coming out of the faucet! At home, the water was always cold, especially in the winter months when it was like ice; it had been terrible. In addition, everyone at home took a bath in a large bucket of water, the same water, and by the time it got to me the water was cold and dirty; you had to skim the dirt off the top.

Here, however, I had the entire tub to myself! I could even add more hot water if it got cold. It was heavenly! I splashed around for the longest time, until finally the Sister told me I had to get out or I would shrivel up like a prune. She smiled at me as she told me that and then she wrapped a large towel around me to dry me off. As she was drying me, she asked, "Helga, where did all of the bruises on your body come from?" I'm not sure what my answer was, but I know I never told on Father.

As she dried me, the Sister told me that from now on I was to take a bath regularly and also wash every day with warm water and soap. I began to look forward to my baths then, and didn't mind washing every day since we had warm water coming right out of the faucet. When I was little, Momma would have warm water ready for me before I got up in the morning. She would heat the water in a pan on the stove. As she got sick, however, a lot of that stopped, and, after she died, I had just stopped washing if I could get away with it.

Once I was all spanking clean and dry, I went back to my room to get dressed. As I was dressing, my thoughts went back to Gela and Helmut. I knew they were all right, but I wanted to see them so badly. Suddenly, I heard crying coming from behind the partition in the back of the room. I hadn't really paid much attention to it before, but now I ran over there thinking that Gela was there. She wasn't, but there was a crib there. In it, was another little girl, who was much older than Gela, maybe four or five years old.

Once I got over my disappointment at not finding Gela, I started feeling sorry for the little girl in the crib. I could not understand why she was kept in that crib, she was pretty big—too big for a crib, I thought. I started talking to her, and she stopped crying. I asked her what her name was and she just looked at me. Curiously, she was not afraid of me. When I was her age, I was afraid of everything. She didn't respond to my questions, and I found out later that she could not speak at all.

Since she had stopped crying, I went back to my bed and finished putting on my new clothes.

It was a really nice outfit. I saw other children later, and they all wore the same clothes. I was just buttoning up my jumper when I heard the little girl crying again. Her crying made me think of Gela again. I knew she was in the orphanage somewhere, but I didn't know where. I wondered how she was and I missed her so. The little girl's crying made me feel so bad for Gela, myself, and the little girl. I went over and climbed into her crib, took her in my arms and rocked her back and forth, crying with her. It was a wonder the bottom of the crib didn't fall out with both of us in it! When finally I looked up, I was scared to find one of the Sisters looking down on both of us. I had not heard her coming into the room, and I was afraid I was going to get punished. To my amazement, she said, "Well, Helga, I see you're getting acquainted with little Ursula." She actually seemed pleased about my being in the crib comforting the little girl. I was so relieved, I cried even more!

As the days went by and I settled in, I came to realize that life in the orphanage was good. I could not believe the kinds and amounts of food we had. While I was there, we ate all kinds of things; we even had an occasional chocolate bar! I heard later that the orphanage was supported by the Americans. Sometimes we saw American trucks stop in front of the orphanage and unload crates and boxes of food. We really received all kinds of goodies. It was especially exciting for me, considering what I had come from, the poverty, the squalor, never knowing whether there was going to be something to eat or not.

Sometimes we met some of the American officers that came to check on the needs of the orphanage. I remember the Sisters introducing me to a nice American officer one day saying, "Now, be sure to curtsey, Helga. The nice man brought us all kinds of fruit." Sure enough, after our nap that afternoon, we were given apples and pears.

I was so relieved to see how wonderful everyone was. No one ever was beaten or severely punished. All of the children were treated with love. I guess I would have been happy if I only had Gela and Helmut nearby, where I could see them. Finally, one day I did see Helmut. I had been playing outside when I spotted him on the other side of the fence, on the other side of the orphanage. He saw me at the same time. We both started to run toward the fence, and, when we got there, I grabbed his hands through the wire. I was so scared that someone would see us and come over and separate us before we could talk. I had not seen him in weeks. The only reason I saw Helmut that day was because one of the Sisters in his wing had lost her rosary and sent several of the boys out to find it after playtime. (The boys' playtime was always different from the girls', even though there was fence between us. As a matter of fact, all of the German schools were segregated—some had only boys; the others had only girls.)

We had just talked for a minute or two when the Sister that was supervising me came over and said, "It's all right if you talk for a few minutes, but then, Helmut, you had better go back in so you won't get into trouble." She left us alone then, and again I could not believe anyone could be so wonderful.

Helmut and I talked for a few more minutes, and he said he missed Gela and me. I told him that I would write Father to come and get us so we could all be together. Helmut said he missed us, but he really did not want to go home. His fear of Father was greater than anything. He even felt that Gela would be safer and better off in the orphanage than at home. Years later, I realized how right he had been.

It really was a good life at the orphanage: No scavenging for scrap metal, no looking for coal, and most of all, no beatings. I had never had it so good! We got up early every morning, washed, had a good breakfast, dressed, and then went off to school.

Since the orphanage was not in Mannheim, but in Schwetzingen, I was going to a new school. I did worse there in my studies, however, than I had before. What made it worse is that I could not read properly. All day in school, all I thought about was getting out. In the orphanage, we had to take a nap every day, and, although I hated naps, they were bearable because we always got a treat like an American chocolate bar or an apple or pear—whatever was in season—after our nap. I loved fruit. I hardly ever had any at home. It seems that my main concerns in life at that time were eating and missing Gela and Helmut. I never did see Helmut again during the few years I was in the orphanage, after those few minutes at the fence.

I became fast friends with the other little girls in my room. Most of them had been there since they were babies. Ursula was kept in the baby bed because she could not be left unsupervised. The Sisters trusted me with Ursula soon, and, when they did not have the time, I was allowed to take her out. The Sisters told me I was the best thing that happened. They called me "Ursula's little mother."

The other girls in my room were all younger than I, except for one girl, who was at least three years older, but she did not act like the others. I could talk to her, and she would listen but she never talked back. I knew she could talk, however, because several times I heard her scream, I woke up expecting something bad to happen. I waited for someone to come and punish her, the way Father used to do to me, but no one came. Apparently the Sisters were used to her. When she had an especially bad night, however, it would wake all of us. Sometimes, it would scare little Ursula so badly, she would cry for hours afterward. Finally, I learned to get up when she first started screaming and turn her around or put my hand on her shoulder, which seemed to calm her. I found out that she had been about six or seven years old when she saw her mother and two sisters get killed in an air raid. Her father was missing in action, so she was the only survivor of her family. When she screamed, I could make out some of the words: "The bombs! The bombs! Watch out. They're coming back!" Other times she would cry out, "Mutti! Hanni!" and another name I could not understand. I could really feel for her as she cried for her family. She never went to school but had someone come in and work with her sometimes. She never changed and never improved while I was there.

She also had terrible burn scars on her body, much worse than mine from the fire. She must have been badly burned to develop those kinds of scars.

We stayed in the orphanage until Christmas of 1952. While we were there, my hair really grew in, even on the bad spots. It was kept short, however, like everyone else's, and never had a chance to grow long. I'm sure they kept everyone's hair short to control lice.

Just before Christmas, Father came and got us. I remember one day the Sister told me that he was to pick me up on the next morning. I could not sleep that night, I was so excited. I would see Gela and Helmut again, after what had seemed like forever. I didn't know how long I had been in the orphanage, but Momma had died in May and Frau Katuck had lived with us from about the end of May until sometime in September. From then on, we had been in the orphanage, which was about 3 years.

I finally went to sleep, but I woke up early, waiting for the six o'clock bell to sound so I could get up and get dressed. When finally it was time to go, I hated to say good-bye to Ursula and the other girls in the room. We had become very close, and little Ursula loved me, I could tell. One of the Sisters ushered me to the visitors' room to wait for Father. It was a teary good-bye with the Sisters too. In that short time, I had come to love them all so much.

The Sisters had to go about their duties and could not sit with me, so I waited there all alone in the visitors' room. I had never been in the visitors' room before; the whole time I was there, I had never had a visitor. Father never came to see us. Finally, there was Father, standing in the doorway, alone. I remember an icy chill coming over me, but I don't know if it was because of him or because he was alone, "Well," he said, "how are you?"

"Fine," I replied, and that was the end of the conversation and we started to go. I did feel better; however, when he told me we were picking up Helmut and Gela as soon as we left my section. I was glad to hear that and felt good knowing they were all right. I had worried about them, something terrible could have happened. I always worried about everything; I do to this day.

It had been such a long time since I had seen Father, but he never hugged me or held my hand—nothing. It was if I had just left the day before. When we got Helmut, he was afraid to hug me too, but he did grab my hand as we walked around to the building to get Gela. Tears were in both our eyes. Then there was the Sister, holding our little sister Gela in her arms. She had changed just a little. She looked as if she had been growing normally and was well fed too. She was getting prettier, too. Her blonde hair was nicely combed and had a little ribbon in it. When we got to her, I expected her to go crazy when she saw us, but when she looked at Father, she turned and clung to the Sister who was holding her, not wanting to go with Father. As he held out his arms to her, she started to cry, so Father just took her and we left.

I was so sad all of the way home. I had expected everything to be so different. I wanted Gela to smile and look at me or hold her arms out to me as she had before, but she whimpered all of the way home. The shock of walking into our old apartment was the worst part. The orphanage had been so nice, with large rooms painted in nice colors and nice beds with good sheets. Our apartment was clean, but the walls had plaster falling from them. Our bed sank in the middle, and then I remembered I would have to sleep in the same bed with father and Helmut and they always kicked me during the night. I did see a crib, however, for Gela.

Then a strange lady walked through the door just as we got there, Father introduced her to us as our new mother, Waltraut. Helmut and I just looked at each other, and I heard Helmut say, "I'm not calling her Momma. My Momma is dead."

I couldn't believe Helmut was saying that, even though I felt the same way, especially after Frau Katuck. I saw Father's face cloud over and got scared. I had not forgotten that look, but Waltraut came to Helmut's rescue and said, "That's all right, Helmut. You're too old to call me Momma. Please call me Waltraut."

Everything went all right that evening, although it took some getting used to, sleeping in the same bed with three others. I guess I'd been spoiled by the orphanage.

There was no escaping it, though; Waltraut was to be our new stepmother. Father had married her while we were in the orphanage. The next morning, I got up early and walked over to Gela's crib. There had not been much time to talk to Gela the day before. I was so busy getting used to being back home. Father, Waltraut, and Helmut were still asleep as I walked over to Gela's crib and said, "Gela, don't you remember me?" When she held out her little arms to me and said "Helga," I knew she remembered me. I was so happy that I cried and I promised her I was going to take care of her, I would not let Waltraut hurt her. I expected Waltraut to be just like Frau Katuck. I was ready for the worst and was prepared to protect that little girl in the crib with my life. I had not seen her for so long, I was not letting her out of my sight!

It was Christmas vacation when Father brought us home from the orphanage, so we could stay home from school, together, for at least a few days. During that time, Helmut, Gela, and I stuck closely together. I completely took over Gela's care. She still could not talk or walk very much, even though she was about three to four years old.

The first thing I did, however, was look for Momma's sweater. I had been unable to take it with me when the social worker picked me up from school to take us to the orphanage. I looked everywhere but could not find it. Then I noticed that none of Momma's things were in the apartment. I could not believe they had just disappeared, especially her sweater; it had seen me through so many nights and days. I had felt like it was a part of Momma. I kept hunting for her things, but the longer I hunted the more worried I became. I finally asked Father what had happened, and he told me that all of Momma's belongings had been sold to a thrift-shop.

I was speechless! If Father had hit me in the stomach as he did before, it would not have hurt as much as losing Momma's sweater. I cried for hours after he told me what he did. That night, after we had all gone to bed, I felt like I had lost Momma all over again. I could not help myself and kept crying. Finally, I heard Father get up. I guessed that my crying was keeping him up. I covered my face with a pillow to muffle the sound.

Father got out of bed and went into the kitchen. I could hear him rummaging around, and I thought, *Oh no, not the foxtail*—the broom handle he used to punish us with. I was terrified as he came over to my side of the bed; the terror made me cry even worse. I remembered, the last time he had beat me with it, Momma had thought I was dead. As Father came toward me, Waltraut shot up in bed to see what was going on; so did Helmut. They both told me later how scared they had been.

Father's voice made me look out from behind my pillow. It was gentle as he said, "Helga, I saved something for you. Give me your hand." I stuck my hand out from under the cover, trembling like a leaf, and Father placed something in the palm of my hand and then gently closed my hand. Father went back to bed, but I just lay there, too scared to look. Father had left a light on so I could see and after getting over the worst of my fear, I slowly opened my hand and found there, wrapped in one of Momma's very own hand-embroidered handkerchiefs, her tiny gold wedding band.

Father had saved it for me. I never could understand Father.

Waltraut, the Stepmother

Waltraut was from Ludwigshaven, a city near Mannheim. She was German. Frau Katuck had been Czechoslovakian. Waltraut was about five feet four and weighed only about 100 pounds. She was a good-looking woman with golden-brown hair.

Father was about forty-plus years old at the time they married, and Waltraut was about twenty-one. I remember being surprised by her good looks and easy smile. From the very first, though, I resolved not to let her get close to me. After Frau Katuck, I was not letting anyone hurt me again. She could beat me, I thought, but she would never hurt me deep inside.

For the first few days we were home from the orphanage, things went well, but after a few days, Father told us that we would have to help earn money again. Now it was back to looking for scrap metal or coal along the river, all of the same things we did before. It was as if nothing had changed, but then I noticed one thing: Waltraut would never tell us what to do. She was totally different from Frau Katuck or my father. I finally realized, also, that she didn't do anything around the house.

Fortunately, I had learned a lot about keeping clean while I was in the orphanage and I started heating water to wash Gela and myself. I even fixed breakfast for Gela, Helmut, and myself, and, to my surprise, Waltraut ate what I cooked. I was also doing all of the cleaning and housekeeping, I even fixed dinner.

When we finally went back to school, nothing got done around the house and Waltraut never told me or asked me to do anything. When Father got home, however, he would beat Waltraut terribly for not making the beds and burning dinner, although I have to admit that dinner looked like an awful mess even before she burnt it!

Going back to school and listening to the other children talk about their Christmas made me realize that Christmas of 1952 had gone by, and none of us had noticed it, not even our new stepmother. That never would have happened had Momma still been alive. I remembered the carols she had taught us and the dolls she had made for me. But most of all, I remembered our trip to the church to hear Christmas Mass. Our church was so beautiful at Christmas. I also missed my beloved Uncle Willi and Aunt Rosel, whom I was not allowed to see. I never saw either of them again. I remember thinking that at least Momma and Uncle Willi would be together in heaven. I treasured the Parcheesi game Uncle Willi had given us the Christmas of 1948 and took it out when I got home from school just to look at it.

As I said, for a few days or weeks things seemed to go along smoothly, except for those few incidents of Waltraut's trying to cook. Then the real trouble started. Father came home one night and found that Waltraut had messed up dinner again, and again he beat her. When I got home from school the next day, the place was in even worse shape and the dinner Waltraut was about to start was unbelievable. I knew that Father would be mad and that he expected her to clean house and fix dinner because I had to go to school. Father also expected me to make money and he knew that I was taking care of Gela and also had homework to do. He knew that I could not take care of everything else. For some reason, however, I felt sorry for Waltraut and I asked her if I could help. When I did that, she broke down and cried as she told me that she did not know how to cook or keep house. When she had been living at home with her family, her chores were all out in the fields, planting, harvesting, feeding chickens and so forth; she had not done any type of work around the house, her mother took care of all of that. Waltraut had not even been allowed in the kitchen.

When Waltraut confided in me and told me how scared she was of Father, she seemed less and less like a threat to me. Soon we became equals, with me almost taking care of her. I would rush home from school every day and try to teach her how to cook, make beds, wash clothes and iron them, but it was no use. No matter how often I showed her how to do these things, she just didn't learn. It was not that she didn't try; she was unable to learn—at times I felt as if I were trying to teach a dog to fly!

Father was also starting to get mad at me for getting behind in my homework, for not earning any money. It was just impossible, though. I had started taking care of Gela from the minute we got home from the orphanage, giving her baths and feeding her before school. Sometimes, it was so much to do that I just could not take it—which made my problems in school even worse. Soon, I was failing in classes. At times I thought I was going crazy, failing school, Father expecting me to earn money, Waltraut helpless, I just didn't know what to do.

Finally, one day I told Waltraut that I couldn't help her in the house because I had to make money. Waltraut told me not to worry, that I should clean the house and cook and she would go out and make money. She did as she promised and a short time later came back with three Deutschmark, which was quite a lot of money. Only rarely had Helmut and I made more than one mark a day hunting for scrap. When I asked her where she worked and how she got the money, she just said, "It's a secret, and don't you tell your father, or he will beat us both." I was only too glad to stay home and cook and clean so Father would not get mad. When I gave Father one mark of the money, he never questioned it. I kept the other two marks for the following two days.

From then on, I kept house and took care of Gela. Every time we ran out of money, Waltraut would go out and return later with two or three marks. On those days that we had money, she would stay at home, talking about all kinds of things. Helmut, in the meantime, spent a lot of time with his friends, friends that I did not know. He stopped helping at home, and he never helped to make any money. Father did not know anything about what was going on and thought that the money I gave him came from our finding scrap.

I'm pretty sure now that Waltraut was making money the only way she knew how. Men always liked Waltraut; she was very pretty. Rather than get a beating from Father, she sold her body so that I could stay at home and do her work. It was funny, all of the things Father used to accuse my real mother of unjustly came true with Waltraut, but yet he never once suspected her of anything. One day I even saw her disappear into our neighbor's house when I knew his wife was working. Later, she returned with three marks as usual, then again stayed home until the money was gone. Fortunately, she never got pregnant but I found out much later that she had been one of the many young girls experimented on by Hitler's doctors, and through whatever they did to her, she was unable to get pregnant. She never talked about it, but I overheard Father telling someone.

Well, things went along, and soon Helmut was fifteen years old. One day, the principal of Helmut's school called Father in and told him that

Helmut was to go to a work farm because he was unmanageable. We had gotten several notices from Helmut's teachers and school personnel, but Waltraut had not shown them to Father. She worried that Helmut would get a beating, so she usually just threw them away.

The juvenile court sent Helmut to a work farm, a private farm. It was terrible without Helmut at home. I knew he was in trouble all of the time, but he loved me and Gela, and he was always good to us. Waltraut had liked him too. He would write to me from the farm and tell me how much he missed Gela and me, but he also wrote that he was happy there. He had made new friends, and the farmer would let him go out on weekends to have fun with his friends. They would also go to church every Sunday.

Except for Helmut's leaving, things did not change much for us the next year, that is, until we were thrown out of our apartment for not paying the rent. Since all of the other people who had lived there had moved out, we had to pay the entire rent alone and couldn't afford it. When we were asked to leave, we were six months behind.

When the day came to move, I thought Father had found us another apartment. I figured it would be smaller or not as nice or something, but I could not believe it when he took Waltraut, Gela and me to our new home! It was in Waldhof and he moved us into a *"Splittegraben,"* in other words, a bunker! The German soldiers had used it for shelter, and it looked like an underground L-shaped corridor. It reminded me of a cement grave!

Poor Waltraut! It was hard enough living the way we had in Mannheim, but now it got even worse. Waltraut and I had grown very close by then, and she loved Gela and me, and we loved her. I hated to see the way Father treated her. Her lovely smile soon disappeared, because she was married to him.

I had finally come to realize that Waltraut had the mentality of an eight-to-twelve year-old, but in some ways she made more sense than Father. I never was able to teach her anything as far as cooking or cleaning, but she could keep secrets and I could tell her things. She protected me from Father in any way that she could. Sometimes, when I think about Waltraut, there are questions, so many questions. I don't know exactly what Hitler's doctors did to her. She was not mentally handicapped; I had met mentally handicapped people and Waltraut was just like everybody else. But there were parts of her brain which would not absorb anything. In years to come, I heard about some of Hitler's experiments. God only knows what was done to her; I did see some scars on her head.

As I think of her, I ask what right did those animals have to destroy a mind? Waltraut was so pretty, so good.

Waltraut left my father at the end of 1955. The last we heard about her, she had married a nice, elderly man who was taking good care of her.

The Bunker

The bunker had no water, no electric lights, nothing. It was a cold, clammy cement hole in the ground with two small openings for windows, which the soldiers must have used to shoot from. It was just big enough to hold a tiny stove, the table and four chairs, and a short sofa-bed, which turned into a double bed at night, and which had been left by the previous occupants. We also had one dresser and another small bed, which was mine. Gela had to sleep with Father and Waltraut.

It was terrible! Waltraut and I cried when we moved in. I don't know how Father found that awful place. It was bad enough that the bunker had no lights, but I'll never forget the embarrassment of having to go to the bathroom in a bucket under a homemade seat and then carrying it upstairs and outside, dig a hole, and bury it. Also, there were no houses next to us so that we had to walk a long way to get water from our closest neighbors. The only good thing about it was that I didn't have to go out looking for scrap, because there were no bombed houses, coal yards, or ships in Waldhof, a small village eight miles from Mannheim.

The best part of it all was that not only did I not have to look for scrap; I did not have to make any money, which meant that Waltraut did not either. I told her that now that we didn't have to worry about money, I would stay home and help her all I could. Waltraut listened to every word I said. I was only thirteen years old then, but I never let her know that I knew what she was doing and how she had made the money. I was only glad that now it would all stop. I really had felt guilty, but I knew there was no other choice for us at the time. If I had not cleaned and cooked for her, she would have gotten a beating, and, if I had made no money,

I would have gotten a beating. We had even been able to buy coal in the winter with the money she had made.

The reason we did not have to worry about making money was that Father did not pay any rent there, and, of course, we had no utility bills. As a result of that, another thing that was better was that we started to have more, and better, food to eat. We had more potatoes and cheese, and even pork once in a while, when we were lucky. When we did, I would make us a pork schnitzel; Momma had taught me to make a delicious schnitzel. We had more flour and eggs, and I was also able to make *Spatzel* (dumplings). I loved cooking, even if Waltraut did get all of the credit. I thought she deserved something, and she was such a kind person; there was nothing that she would not do for me. Father never knew who did the cooking. On weekends or anytime that he was around, I just pretended that I was helping her while she went through the motions. I even baked a delicious *Ruhrkuchen* (bundt cake).

There were some good times in the bunker, but they were few and far between. At times, we had no money at all, especially at the end of the month. It was summer when we moved into the bunker, and, while it was terrible, we didn't think it could get any worse. Were we surprised, however, when winter really set in. The winter of 1953 was something else. During the summer we had not noticed all of the cracks and holes through which the wind and air could pass. The outside of the bunker consisted of old planks of wood nailed together, and the windows had holes all around them. Even though they were tiny, it was unbelievable how much cold could come through.

When it started to snow, it became even worse. Water ran down the stairway and formed puddles on the floor in front of my bed. It was difficult to use the handmade toilet because of the cold. We had had to sell our large stove when we moved, and all we had for heat was a small stove. It was so small that you practically had to stand on it before you could feel any heat.

The worst thing, though, was the water. The walls were seeping water all winter long, much like an unfinished basement today, only worse. All of the furniture was pushed next to the walls to allow us room to walk by, so it too, was damp and wet. I remember that my *Fedderbettcover* (down comforter) got completely damp, keeping me clammy all winter long. One morning when I woke up, all four corners of my *Fedderbettcover* were frozen stiff, even though we had had the stove burning all night. It was too small, though, to make a difference.

One other morning, when I woke up, I slipped and fell getting out of bed. The floor of the bunker was frozen over with a one-inch-thick mass of ice. The little stove had gone out during the night, and even the walls were frozen. I was unable to wash because the water in our water bucket had frozen through. Even though I tried, I could not break enough ice with the ice pick to melt and heat for washing and breakfast. I remember going to school that morning and wishing that I was back in Mannheim. I missed my school there and I missed my church, the beautiful Evangelist Christuskirch in Mannheim. Here I was to be fourteen years old in January and was to be confirmed in March. I was afraid that I would not make it because I was missing so much time from school and church that winter because of the conditions in the bunker. Father did finally put down some old wooden planks on the floor so that the water would not touch our feet or furniture and so that, when it froze, we would not slip on the ice. It was so embarrassing when people found out where we lived.

My poor sister Gela was sick all winter long, with a cough and a runny nose. One winter morning I found her laying uncovered in bed; she was all cold and blue looking. Father and Waltraut had all of the bed covers on their side. From then on, I started to put her in my bed on the really cold days so she would not get sick or die. I had finally learned to move my bed away from the wet wall during the night (I would move it back in the morning) and to keep my bed-covers away from the wall.

So many other things happened while we were there in the bunker. Gela started school, and I walked with her every morning. One of the main events was that, since Waltraut had married my father, most of the beatings stopped. She had a way about her, like a little girl but yet all woman. I knew by then that she could not read or write, but she had learned how to keep Father from hitting her or me. Anytime Father would get angry, she would say, "Adam, it is that time of the month" (meaning that she was having her menstrual period). That would always stop Father cold. If Father was angry with me, she would step in and say, "Adam, Helga has her period," even if I did not; I certainly didn't correct her when she was wrong. I guess that after Momma had bled to death, Father was scared of any kind of blood. I was glad of that. Waltraut got me out of several beatings that way.

There was one thing she could not get me out of, however. Father had started to repair shoes for us and the neighbors to make money. Every Saturday, he would get out his hammer and fix shoes. That in itself was not bad; the problem was that he expected me to hold all of the nails as he hammered them into the shoes. I did not mind at first, but, when he missed, he hit *my* fingers! Soon, I was so scared to hold the nails that I shook before he even hammered them. That would make him mad and he would scream, "Hold still!" When it was impossible for me to stop shaking, he would hit me in the face. I tried so hard to hold those nails still but the tears in my eyes clouded my vision, then *wham*! He hit my hand so hard that both my thumb and forefinger swelled up and turned blue. Later, both fingernails came off at the root. After that, he had Gela holding the nails.

Gela was about seven or eight years old then. I felt sorry for her; I knew how scared she was. I wanted to help, but Father decided that Gela was a better nail-holder, which she was. Gela was a feisty little girl, but I know Father scared her.

At some point, Father got a job at the movie theater in Waldhof and he would work late a lot of the nights. After Father had treated Waltraut especially bad, she started to go out the nights when he worked. I don't know where she went, but I had a feeling. I would watch the clock, hoping she would come back before Father got home. I think he would have killed her had he known.

In the meantime, she was wonderful to both Gela and me. We all got along fine; she acted no older than twelve. Everything she tried to do was hard for her except for being kind to others. She had a heart full of love for everyone. It was hard to believe that I could show her how to sew on a button one day, and the next she would not remember how to do it. She looked so intelligent, and she acted intelligent, but her head was empty. Sometimes, we would talk for hours; then later I realized it was mostly me doing all of the talking, and she just agreed with whatever I said. The next day, she did not even remember the conversation. I realized that she was never going to change, so I just left things the way they were. She was clean; she kept herself very clean, taking hours just to wash and get ready in the morning, as if someone had taught her, step-by-step, what to do. She did the same thing every morning down to the exact detail. When she had finished getting dressed, that was it for the day until the next morning. I don't know how she acted with men, I guess the same as she did around Father. She just smiled and kept quiet, although her smile disappeared later in her marriage to Father. Father had a wife, but that was about all. I loved her as if she were a little sister.

In the meantime, Gela was growing up without a real mother. I tried to be like Momma, but I guess at age thirteen I was not quite old enough to be the mother she needed. Growing up without a mother had turned Gela into a tough little girl. I used to watch her at school, getting into fights with boys twice her size—Gela usually won! I would find out later the reason for the fight was to defend the family's honor or to defend me when someone had called me a bad name or talked about where we lived. (Soon the entire school knew this anyway.) I sometimes watched her play outside the bunker among the wildflowers growing out of the little hills where we had buried our sewage. I didn't know how much I could take. Momma would never have let us live in a place like that. My beautiful little sister was being raised as a tomboy, getting into all kinds of scraps, and most of the time starting them herself. I knew Momma would have made pretty little dresses for her, fixed her hair as she had mine, and probably have gotten rid of her chronic runny nose by taking her to a doctor. I don't think Gela was ever to a doctor from the time Father had gotten her out of the hospital. None of us went. It's a wonder we all did not get sick while living in the bunker.

Father was the only one that did have any type of illness while we were there and he caught pneumonia. He also had bronchitis. Of course, that might have been from smoking two packs of cigarettes a day. At least, as he used to say, he did not "drink like some other guys." He was right there; I never saw my father drunk.

There were some happy times in the bunker. After a while, Helmut started to come home from the farm to visit on weekends. He even brought friends with him, who really liked me. We all had fun together. Since Father was working at the movie house, we would get passes from him and go to the movie. Or we would stay home and play games. I could see that Helmut's friends were shocked at the way we lived, but Helmut did not care. He told me later in a letter that both of his friends had "taken a shine" to me. One even started to write to me, but Father would now allow me to write back.

Helmut had come home several times before the big fight. Helmut was almost seventeen years old that day when he came. Father got mad about something, but this time Helmut did not keep quiet, but actually started to argue with Father. Father grabbed a large butcher knife and started after Helmut. Fortunately, Helmut was much faster than Father. I know that if Father had caught up with Helmut, Helmut would have been dead, just like Uncle Willi. Thank God, Helmut was fast. Helmut would not speak to Father after that. It was almost ten years before they spoke to each other again.

Time went by as we lived in that bunker. I was confirmed, and I graduated from middle school. I started high school July 1, 1954, and my days became busier than ever. I would go to school from 8:00 A.M. until 12 noon, so I had to get up early to help clean the bunker. Along with starting high school, I also started working at a job in Mannheim from 1:00 P.M. to 5:00 P.M., so I really had to hustle, because it was a forty-five-minute bike ride from school to work on the outskirts of the city, by the river. After work, I had to hurry home to help fix dinner.

I was working as an apprentice. The place where I worked would teach you any type of skill or trade, from saleslady to executive, but you first had to put in your time as an apprentice for the required number of years. After a certain amount of time, the concern would then decide what you were qualified for. My concern was one of the largest in Mannheim. I had been lucky to have been chosen as one of the "hirelings," as they called us. I was chosen because of my grades in school, which had become much better by then. I liked working there and I learned a lot, but it took such a long time to get from one place to the other, even by bicycle. It took me twenty minutes to get to school and, from school, it was forty-five minutes to work.

Thank goodness I could eat at the *Konsumgenossenscheft* (cafeteria) before starting to work. I loved the food there, and the money to pay for it was deducted from my paycheck. That was fine with me, because I never saw my check anyway. Father took every cent of it.

It was another forty-five-minute ride from work to home, and I dared not be late. Father had never worried about how late I would get home when I was younger, hunting for scrap. But now, since I had turned fourteen and developed a nice figure, I had to account for every minute of my time. A friend of my father's had noticed the change too, and one day, he approached me and made advances to me. When I turned him down, he swore he would get even with me. I didn't tell Father about the incident, but I later wished I had.

Coming home from work one day, I had trouble with my bicycle chain, and I was ten minutes late arriving home. Father's friend was there, and, when Father mentioned to him I was late, he took the opportunity to get even with me by telling Father that he had seen me chatting with some friends, which was a lie. Then, when I finally told Father about the chain, he not only beat me for being late, but also for lying to him. From then on, I knew that I had to watch out for that man. I wanted never to be late again. I pushed myself so hard, I would come home sweating.

Then it happened. I was getting ready to leave from work to go home, and I had a flat tire. I knew that I was going to be late. It was a forty-five-minute bike ride, and I didn't know how long it was going to take walking. I had no way of getting help or getting in touch with Father to let him know where I was; there were no telephones. I knew that it would be dark.

I had no choice but to walk. As I walked, I thought that Father would believe me when he saw the flat. I had tried to pump it up, but I needed a new tire. I just knew he would believe me, but then I started thinking, *what if he doesn't? No, No,* I thought, *I can't let myself get scared. I have done nothing wrong.*

I walked and I walked. It was almost dark when I got near the bunker. I had almost talked myself into not worrying, when out from behind the bunker door darted Gela. She ran right at me, yelling, "Run! Run!"

I knew something was wrong, so I just dropped my bike and I ran. Gela followed behind me. After I noticed that no one was following, I stopped and asked Gela, *"Was ist los?"* She told me that Father's friend had come to visit and told Father he had seen me hours ago, taking off with a boy. I was shocked. Gela told me that when Father heard that, he started to get madder than she had ever seen him in her life. She begged me, "Please don't go down there. He will kill you. Waltraut was unable to calm him down and told me to get water from the neighbor. She knew that would give me a chance to warn you."

It was April 26, 1955. I did not know what to do. I had no clothes, just what I was wearing. I had no money. The fear of my father was too great so I ran away from home. I ran as far as I could, and then I found shelter for the night in the hallway of an apartment house.

The New Beginning

All night long, I wondered where I would go, what I would do. I knew that if I went to the police, they would just take me home or maybe worse put me on a farm or in a home for juvenile delinquents. The government was really strict with underage children, and I had just turned fifteen in January. I remember praying for an answer. I knew that I could not go back home. No matter what might happen to me, it could not be any worse than the beatings, the fear, the coldness or having no money and no proper clothes. Worst of all, Father would never leave that bunker; I knew that for a fact. A social worker had approached Father once and told him that we were eligible for a low-rent apartment. I had seen them; they were gorgeous, in a well-kept three-story building, with balconies, in Mannheim, near everything. I almost cried when I heard him say that he would stay in the bunker until he died. Waltraut, Gela, and I were not even consulted.

Well, I decided, I was not going back to the bunker. I finally remembered that there was a village of American families in Käfertal. I walked there the next morning, not knowing what I was going to do, only knowing that I had a feeling about the Americans.

Käfertal was a small village of nice houses with playgrounds filled with children playing. It was almost 9:00 A.M. or 10:00 A.M. when I got there. I walked from house to house, just looking at them and admiring how nicely they were kept. *What could I say?* I wondered. *What would these Americans think of me? A runaway, what can I offer to them?*

Finally it came to me: I knew how to keep house and take care of children; I would offer my services as a housekeeper. That was it! Upon reaching that decision, I walked up to several houses and knocked at the door. When the lady of the house answered, I explained that I was looking for a job and what I could do. Most of the American women were wonderfully nice, but none of them could speak German. I was unable to get through to them, I had forgotten about the language barrier. I was getting really discouraged when I finally came to a house where instead of the lady trying to talk to me, she called for someone. In just a moment, her husband came to the door, and it turned out that he spoke German very well. He took one look at me, and asked me into the house.

Their name was Graves, and he was a master sergeant in the U.S. Army. They were an older couple and were so wonderful. Mrs. Graves first fixed me something to eat, and we sat in the kitchen talking. As we talked, Sgt. Graves translated everything for his wife. I didn't mean to do it, but, before long, everything came out. I told them that I was a runaway, and that I was so scared to go home. I begged them not to turn me in. They promised they would not, but Sergeant Graves told me that, although my father would have to be told, I would not have to go home; they would protect me. He soon left with a driver to talk to my father.

In the meantime, Mrs. Graves took me upstairs. There were several rooms up there, and she showed me into one of them. When we walked in, I saw two children playing there on the floor, a boy and a girl. She pointed at the boy, saying "Paul—four years" as she held up four fingers. Then she pointed to the girl, raised three fingers, and said, "Linda—three years." They were the cutest children. When they saw me, Paul gave me a big smile, and so did Linda. What really stunned me, though, was that the children spoke German! I thought I was mistaken at first, but they could not speak one word of English—just like me. When Sergeant Graves returned, I found out that Mrs. Graves could not have children and that they had adopted these two German children just weeks before I got there.

Sergeant Graves was gone less than two hours, and, when he returned, he took Mrs. Graves aside, and they talked seriously for quite some time. She looked terribly unhappy, shaking her head no, now and then, as she looked over to me. I could not understand one word, but I thought there was going to be trouble with Father and that I would have to go home. Just then, Mrs. Graves came over to me and, surprisingly, put her arm around me. I was not used to any kind of affection, especially from a stranger, and I stiffened under her touch. She held onto me though, as if she were trying to protect me. As she held me, she started talking to me and he translated.

"Helga," he was saying, "my wife and I have just adopted these two German children. Since my wife can't speak German, she would love for you to come and live with us. You could help with the children. We know they miss having someone to talk to them in German."

When he said they would love to have me come and live with them, I broke out in tears; so did Mrs. Graves, who was still holding me. Sergeant Graves hugged both of us; he was crying too. Sergeant Graves never told me what happened at my father's house.

Living with the Graves was a whole new life. I had my own room, and the children soon loved me, and I, them. Mrs. Graves was a hardworking lady. Her house was spotless. I did my best to help her clean the house, fix dinner, iron clothes, and help with the children she loved so dearly. She loved me too and actually expected very little of me. I became one of her daughters in every respect. I was given a large allowance, and Mrs. Graves made me new dresses. Sergeant Graves helped me to learn English. They even took me to their church, and soon I belonged to their church choir. Although my English was still not good, singing in English seemed to be easy. They were so proud of me as they often told me.

I did have to give up my job as an apprentice; it was just too far from the Graves' house. Besides, they told me I would not need it, that I was to be one of their girls. They told me there was still plenty of time to go to work when I turned sixteen.

I could not believe the life I was leading. It was heaven—good food, a beautiful room, my own two dresses, and a closet. The Graves had a lovely bathroom with hot running water, fluffy towels, and soap that was the most amazing thing. The Graves bought expensive soap, not the brown lye soap we had used. They also had shampoo for my hair. After I used it, I was so surprised at how nice my hair looked; it had all kinds of highlights I had never seen before. At home, we would buy one large bar of lye soap, and it was used for everything—from scrubbing floors to washing dishes to washing hair and face!

The Graves also had a washer in the basement and central heat. There was an icebox filled with food, but best of all, they had an electric stove for cooking. I really liked that stove; no one had to watch it and it would not get the house all black and sooty. I also loved doing the dishes in their large sink! It really was an entirely new life. I discovered more new things every day.

I would have been totally satisfied if it had not been for Gela. She still lived in that bunker. I could not feel sorry for Father however; he had been offered a nice place to live. When I knew that Father would not be there, I started to go home to visit Gela. I visited her quite often, especially during school vacation. Mrs. Graves always packed me something to take to Gela.

The Graves had made sure that I went to school, and everything seemed to be going along so well. Soon there was talk of adopting me, and I really was in heaven! It was everything I had ever dreamed of—a family of my own. I was walking around on cloud nine, but then I found out we were to soon go to the United States. I was shocked!

I had never dreamed that sooner or later the Graves would have to return to the US. I guess I thought they lived in Käfertal for good. I did not know what to do or to think. I wanted to be with the Graves, but I kept thinking of Gela. How could I leave my sister? My heart was sad, I knew that I could not go without Gela and remembered my promise to my mother.

One day, Sergeant Graves came home looking very sad. He told me that he had been to visit my father to get his permission for my adoption, but Father had turned him down. He seemed more upset than I. I felt that it was just as well, because I could not stand the idea of leaving Gela behind.

When it came time for the Graves to leave for America, saying good-bye was the hardest thing I had ever had to do. They were such wonderful people, and I had come to love them and the children so much. I had felt a security with the Graves that I had never felt before in my life. They had given me something more than that, though; they had made me believe in myself. The Graves had introduced me to a nice family before they left, who were to give me room and board in exchange for my helping to clean the house and babysitting on weekends. I also found another job in a bakery, part time. I knew that, with the Graves gone, I would have to support myself.

I was almost seventeen years old when the Graves left, still underage. Father had not bothered me while I lived at the Graves'. I did not know what he would do now. Luckily, he did not do anything and never bothered me. My fear of him, however, stayed with me day after day.

The other family was very nice, but I soon found out that I would never be considered a member of the family. I was given the maid's room in the attic. I still had to go to school in the morning, and now, in the afternoon, I worked at the bakery. I would get up early Saturday morning to do the laundry or wash floors or windows or whatever my new employer wanted. I also would get up early Sunday and fix breakfast for the family and sometimes babysit all day or all night, which left very little time for a social life of my own, but I was glad that I had a place to live.

It was a lovely room up in the attic. The window overlooked the entire village. I could see the children playing in sandboxes or swinging on the swing sets. When I saw them, my thoughts would turn to Gela. I could just see her playing on top of the bunker, scrapping with all of the neighborhood boys and getting bloody noses from Father, or maybe worse from holding nails.

Finally the day came, and I went to the bunker. I was so scared; I did not know what would happen. I should not have worried. When I got there, there sat Father, in the bunker, smoking his cigarette, acting as if I had just left minutes ago. It had been two years. He never mentioned anything, and neither did I. We spoke very little. I never did understand Father.

After that, I was able to have Gela come and visit me. Sometimes she would stay with me overnight in my room; she liked that. She even started to come over on Father's bicycle. Father never bothered me anymore, especially after I started to buy him things or bring him food to eat. I even started to give him money. He was working then, but I knew that he made very little money. I didn't have much either, only what I made at my part-time job, but I didn't need much money. Mrs. Graves had sewn some lovely clothes for me, and I had my room and board. All I needed money for was to buy an occasional tire for my bike or to buy shampoo or soap. My needs were few. I found a lovely thrift shop in our American village, where I bought Gela some nice things too. I always remembered birthdays and Christmas, and whatever was left after that, I gave to Father.

I remember one Christmas I had saved all of my paychecks for weeks and weeks ahead of time to be able to buy presents for Gela and Father. I still remember the small twinge of pain I got, however, when I realized that Father had not gotten me anything for Christmas. I knew he could have afforded a card or maybe even a handkerchief, but, then, I hadn't gotten a present since Momma had died. Momma had always taken care of things like that, and she had made sure that no matter how rough things were, Helmut and I still got something.

I remember that last Christmas at the Graves', and what they did when they learned that I would not be able to accompany them to the United States; they had bought me all kinds of stuff for Christmas, things that I would need. They had given me four large towels and four washcloths, all in a beautiful yellow. There was also a handkerchief, still wrapped in its box and about a year's supply of the expensive soap. I was also given a supply of shampoo and toothpaste and even a small first-aid kit with bandages. (I used a lot of them on my feet!) The box also contained aspirin, scissors, and a beautiful comb, brush and mirror set. They even gave me a box of stationery and stamps. I remember Mrs. Graves had cried when she told me to write to her. I guess she had forgotten that I could not write English.

Now that I was taking stuff to Father and Gela all of the time, I felt like Santa Claus. It made me feel good to be good to them. It seemed as if they just waited for me to show up, but as long as Gela was happy, that was all that mattered.

As I grew older, my thoughts of Gela were eating me up. I felt guilty leaving her in that bunker. I wished there was some way that I could get that skinny little girl out of there. Her face looked so much like Mother's. I was often told that I was the image of my mother, but that was because I had blonde hair and blue eyes as she had. I knew that I was really the image of my father. I had his nose and the shape of his face. He also had blue eyes. I was praying in the depths of my soul that I would never be like him.

I even had the Braun body. Where Momma had been little, tiny even, with delicate features, I was about five feet three inches tall and weighed about 118 pounds. I didn't think my father was ugly; I guess he had been considered a very attractive man in his time. He wasn't tall, but he had a good head of black wavy hair, those blue eyes, and a slim body. What I did hate about him, though, was those large hands. Judging from his hands, you would have thought he was six foot seven; they were so big. Those hands could hurt a child, they could hurt a child badly.

I would be upset for days after seeing Gela; she was so little and so like Momma in miniature. Momma's sad eyes were begging me to take her home with me each time, it seemed. What could I do? Thank goodness Helmut was safely on the farm. I always asked Gela if Father was treating her all right. She never complained, but would say, "You know how it is." I was hoping that Father had changed. She was so tough, that innocent little girl.

One Sunday, however, she had a black eye. I asked her what had happened, and she said Father had been out the night before. It was cold outside, and Gela knew that his bed would be cold when he got home (she slept in my old bed now), so she warmed a brick in the oven, wrapped a towel around it, and put it into his bed to warm it. (This was a method we had used for years.) Evidently he was not used to having Gela do that for him; she was trying to surprise him. When Father got home and went to bed, I guess he hurt himself on the brick, which made him so mad; he hit Gela in the face while she was asleep. I remembered how that felt; he had done the same to me dozens of times. I had nightmares after Gela told me about that. I woke up several times in a cold sweat expecting Father to beat me too.

One day, Gela told me that Father was having "attacks." She said that he would be sitting on his chair, and all at once his face would get a funny look; then he would go slack and he would fall on the floor. He had been to the doctor, she said, but there was nothing that could be done about it. Gela said she was already getting used to it. He was too heavy for her to lift, so she would just cover him up. I started to worry about how long it would be before Gela got sick.

I started dating that year. Most of the guys I dated did not mind taking Gela with us on a Sunday drive or to an occasional movie. I loved taking her with me. I used to call her my little chaperone.

I graduated from high school on April 6, 1957. I was at the top of my class. When I got out of school, I started working full time at the PX, since I spoke English. I also still worked for an American family in exchange for room and board, but it was a different couple, with no children. They were in the same building, but they were much less demanding than the other family, and I had more time to myself. The new couple made me work only on Saturday and do all the dishes after all the meals.

It was funny about the guys I dated. A lot of them only dated me one time, then never came back for a second date, or, if they did, they asked me to marry them. I only dated Americans. I had seven marriage proposals by the time I was eighteen years old. I could not understand why so many guys never came back for a second date, and I guess that hurt my feelings. As one guy put it, though, "Helga, you are too nice of a girl; most of us guys are only after one thing." Well, I knew what he meant, although no one had ever talked to me about things like that. I felt I should save myself for the man I married. Well, I sure was not thinking of marriage, though. I had seen family life, and I did not want any part of it. I didn't really know what I wanted out of life or what to do about my future.

My concern was to make enough money to be able to get a place of my own and have Gela come and live with me for good. It was all right to date, but I was not about to have a husband knock me around the way I had seen Father hit Mother.

By that time, Helmut had moved back to Mannheim to be closer to Gela and me. He was twenty years old then and worked at a furniture store during the day and as a drummer at night. He had left the farmer with regret. He had come to love the farmer and his wife, who, he said, treated him like a son. They had even let him take music lessons while he was there. He was only supposed to have stayed with them until he was eighteen, but the farmer persuaded him to stay an extra two years.

I remember the day Helmut came to visit me after leaving the farm. After that incident with Father, he had stayed away for almost three years, and, although we had stayed in touch by letter, I had not seen him. I had missed him terribly. When I answered the door that day, I did not recognize the tall, good-looking man standing there; he was six foot two; his hair still golden blonde, and his blue eyes were twinkling at me. He weighted about 185 pounds. I could not believe it—the last time I had seen him, he was a pimply, gangly, skinny beanpole, and now he looked like a movie star. He was better looking than James Dean. I was so proud of my big brother. He lifted me up and swung me around. We had a wonderful visit.

The only thing that bothered Helmut was the fact that I was dating. From that time on, he tried to take me with him every weekend when he played in a band for the USO. It really turned out great for me. As far as Helmut was concerned, no one really was good enough for his little sister! I loved the interest he showed in my social life.

Helmut played for the USO every Saturday evening from five until ten. It was wonderful! I was with him and I got to meet hundreds of GIs, although I was not allowed to date them. The USO had a no-dating rule, and I had to go home with the band. Sometimes I was asked to sing or dance with the GIs, but mostly these lonely guys would sit with me and talk about their families back home and how lonely they were. I felt so good about being there for them; they could have gone to bars in Mannheim and picked up girls, but a lot of them had a girlfriend or wife and children at home. They wanted desperately to be faithful to them. I could feel it. Most of those soldiers were stationed there for two years, which was a long time to have no one to talk to except for the others in the barracks.

There were several hostesses at the USO. They served coffee and donuts, free of charge. Helmut's band also donated its time, and I was considered a part of the band. While we were there, I had dozens of soldiers tell me their problems. I saw dozens of pictures of girlfriends, wives, and children from back home. It was probably one of the best times of my life.

Then I met Tony. He was a soldier also. I met him at a dance I had gone to with some friends. He told me that he had seen me for a long time at the USO, but he was aware of the USO rules and had not come up to talk to me. He asked me for a date the next day, which was a Sunday. It was okay to date out of the USO.

0I was shocked the next day, though. He had seemed like such a nice man at the dance, but when he showed up at 2:00 P.M. in the afternoon for our date, he was drunk. I told him that I was not about to go out with someone drunk like that! I found out later that he was so nervous. He had drunk a few beers to give himself courage before picking me up. He told me later that he had loved me from the first day he had seen me, one year before, in the USO, but he had never believed that he could ever get a date with me; there were always soldiers around me, although he knew that I did not date any of them.

Well, he seemed like such a nice guy, other than being drunk, that I told him to go back to the barracks and sober up. He said he would if I would go out on a date with him that evening. I agreed and met him at 7:00 P.M. He was sober.

Tony took me to a little restaurant that he frequented at the time. I ordered a Coke, and so did he. We talked for hours. He was different from a lot of the men I had dated. He never bragged. As a matter of fact, he told me that his family was poor. He sent money home each month to help out. His father was from Italy and had immigrated to the United States in 1905. His mother was English and French. I remember his telling me that they would love me.

It had been a wonderful date. I liked him instantly. He was not very tall, but he had a head full of black curly hair and warm brown eyes. What had impressed me most about him was his honesty. Still. I was shocked when, that first evening, he asked me to marry him. I remember his exact words. He said, "Helga, I'm not rich, but I will work hard to make a good life for you. I will always be good to you, and I will never let anything or anyone hurt you, including myself."

I told him he was crazy, but I accepted his proposal two weeks later, and we were married soon after that. It was only to be a small wedding with one of his friends as best man. Helmut could not make it because he was out of town on work. My Father and Gela were also invited to the wedding. Tony had met Gela a few days before, and he had loved her instantly. He also liked my father. Father was on his best behavior with Tony. He seemed to be different with Tony. I could see that Tony really liked my family, and it was not an act. I never took Tony to the bunker though; I would have been too embarrassed. I always met him at the village where I was working and had my room. He would wait outside for me, and then we would meet Gela or Father elsewhere.

It was a very short wedding at the courthouse. Tony never even got to kiss the bride! There was an interpreter there to translate the quick ceremony, because Tony could not speak German.

Before we got married, Tony had rented a nice little apartment on a farm. It was just a little two-room apartment inside the farmhouse, but I was tickled with it, and it was just a few minutes from Tony's army post. We planned to move in there right after a short honeymoon in the Black Forest. Actually, it was more like an outing than a honeymoon. We were only to be gone one day.

When Tony watched Gela as she was getting ready to leave, sad faced, for home after the ceremony, he said, "Wait a minute," and took me aside, "Why don't we take Gela and your father with us?" he asked. "It would do them good to get out a little." I knew right there and then that I had not made a mistake by marrying this kindhearted man.

Well, we took Gela and Father with us on our honeymoon, funny as that may sound. We had a wonderful time. Tony had bought an old 1949 Mercedes that looked as if it was about to fall apart, but happily it never broke down. It was even a convertible. I remember he had paid fifty dollars for it. It was the month of August, and the weather was wonderful. We had the top down as we drove off. I still remember eating potato salad and *Wiener Wuerstchen* that night for dinner and Gela making Tony stop along a country road somewhere. She had spotted some apple trees along the road and, before I could stop her, she had already picked some for the four of us. I remember thinking to myself that that tomboy would never change.

When we got home I asked Father to let Gela come and live with me, but he said no. He did, however, let her spend a lot of time with us. The farm was not too far from Waldhof, and Gela would come over on Father's bike. She spent her summer vacation with us, and Father came to visit too. I asked him several more times to let Gela live with us, but the answer was always the same. As Gela put it, "He just wants me to help him. Who would get the water for him? Who would help cook? Who would mind the stove in the winter while he is out running around?"

Father had quite an eye for the ladies. Gela told me that, after Waltraut had left, he had brought quite a few other women home with him, but none of them stayed. It bothered me terribly that there was no way I could get Gela away from Father. In the meantime, I just enjoyed the time I did have with her.

Helmut also came to see us; he was so sorry he had missed the wedding, but his job was more important. Good jobs were hard to come by then. Helmut and Tony got along well. Helmut approved of my choice of husband, as he told me himself.

Finally it was time for Tony to go back home to the USA. He had been in Germany for three years (he had gotten a one year extension to stay), but now he had to re-enlist or go home. There was no other way. Just three months before we left, we had our first little girl. We named her Sylvia. Gela was ecstatic when I got back home from the hospital. Tony told me she had come with her bicycle every day to see if I was home yet. She was not allowed in the hospital because she was too young and the baby had to be born in the army hospital because Tony was an American citizen.

Gela loved little Sylvia, and soon she learned how to change a diaper and feed the baby. Every chance she got, Gela wanted to take care of Sylvia; she was just like a little mother! It was so good to see them together. At first I was skeptical, Gela was such a tomboy, but soon enough I found she was as good with Sylvia as I was. I also saw a change come over Gela. With some of the clothes I had bought for her in the beginning, she was starting to look and act more like a little lady each day—well, almost.

One day I had to run out to get some milk. I came back to the loudest shouting match I had ever heard. It was Gela and my landlady! My landlady had been a wonderful woman, always peeking in on little Sylvia and begging me to let her pick her up. I was reluctant to let her do so because, although she was one of the nicest women I knew, she was not the neatest. Working out in the fields all day as she did, she never washed her hands until suppertime. Well, Gela was aware of that too, and apparently the landlady had come in while I was gone, wanting to see the baby. Gela had told her, in no uncertain terms, that she was not going to let her touch Sylvia. With that, the fight erupted.

"Who are you to tell me what I can't do? You're just a little girl yourself!" the landlady was yelling.

Gela was yelling back, at the top of her lungs, "But I wash my hands first before I come near the baby! Don't you know anything about babies?"

I couldn't help but grin to myself as I walked into the apartment. I had always found excuses for not letting the landlady know why I would not let her hold Sylvia, but here Gela told her how it was. As I walked into the apartment, she brushed past me saying, *"Grüss Gott."*

I walked into the bedroom and there stood Gela, hands on her hips. She lit up as she saw me and said, "I told her, huh?"

I just laughed. I guessed that one of those days I would have to teach Gela about manners, but that was not the day!

Well, the day of parting finally came. It was a black day when we left Germany. I was worried that I would never see Gela again. I had no other choice but to leave her with Father. My only hope was that she would be of age in another six years, and then I could send for her. It was hard saying good-bye to Helmut too. I knew, however, that he could take care of himself. He also promised me he would come to visit me, a promise he later kept when, in 1969, he came to visit for six weeks.

On July 19, 1959, Tony, Sylvia, and I arrived in Maryland. I was so homesick for Germany though. Germany had almost rebuilt itself by the time I left. I had known sooner or later that I would have to go home with Tony, but I guess it never really hit me until we were here in the States.

Tony took me to all kinds of places. Our home was in Frederick, Maryland, which was the perfect place to raise children. Living in Frederick, we were close to Washington, D.C., and Baltimore. We visited all of the places around, and I knew it was beautiful, but it was not home to me just yet. I didn't realize it at the time, but Gela had become just like my own child. What mother can leave her own child? I just couldn't get used to the United States without her. Tony just kept assuring me that we would get her someday. Well, someday was a long, long way off, six years—I thought it was a lifetime away. As time passed, I grew very homesick.

Tony had been right about his parents, though. I loved them from the very start. I could not believe what a warm, close family they were. Pop and Mom, as I called them, took me under their wing. Over the years, they were to love me as much as Tony. It was an entirely new life for me. I did my best to be the wife Tony wanted and never once regretted marrying him.

Then the letters started coming from Gela. We had left Germany in 1959. My father wrote sometimes, but now Gela had started to write about how things were getting worse at home. In one letter, she said she was about to run away from home. She was still only twelve years old. It was not like Gela to complain like that. She was pretty tough and I wondered what was going on over there. She was living alone with Father down in that bunker, and I was worried.

I talked to Tony about the situation and, without even thinking about it, he said, "Why don't we send for her?"

"Father would never let her go," I said. Tony insisted that maybe now he would. I sat down, then, and wrote the longest letter to Father, almost begging him to let Gela come and live with me. I wrote how much I missed her and mailed the letter off.

It was terrible waiting for the mailman. Finally it came: a letter from Father. My hands trembled so that I could hardly open it. As I read his letter, I was dismayed. He had written me that we could send for Gela, but only if we sent for him too. My heart sank. I told Tony the bad news the minute he got home. Again, Tony proved to be the most wonderful man in the world. He said, "If he wants to come too, that's fine. We'll send for both of them."

I could not believe he would want them both. Where would we get the money? To send for a person, you have to prove that you are going to be responsible for their housing, food, medical, and schooling. Tony didn't care; there was nothing he wouldn't do for me. He had seen how much I missed Gela.

The very next day, Tony took off from work and we saw a lawyer to make all of the arrangements. We then went to a bank to borrow money for Gela's and Father's visa and airplane tickets and inoculations. I think Tony would have moved mountains to make me happy.

Finally the day came, and we were to pick them up at the Dulles Airport. I was thinking about the big surprise I would have for Gela. Just six weeks earlier I had given birth to a second baby girl, whom we had named Angela after my sister. I wanted to take little Angie with me to the airport, but we did not know how long it would take, so we had left her with Tony's mother. But there we were, Tony, Sylvia, and I waiting anxiously. When I saw them getting off the plane, they looked exactly as they had the day I left!

Gela was a little taller, but that was all. She was just as skinny as when I left her, maybe a little skinnier. I just looked at her, tears streaming down my face. Tony was holding onto my hand and had Sylvia in his arms, but still managed to wave to them with me. They saw us and waved back. I saw the look on Gela's face and knew that it had been worth all of the trouble and expense to bring her over, and Father too.

It did not take long at the customs counter. The inspector took one look at the contents of Father's suitcase and slammed the lid down, pushed it toward Father, and said, "Next." I was somewhat surprised that it went so quickly, but I soon found out why. Gela told me later that she had told Father not to bring those moldy sheets or anything else from the bunker, but he would not listen to her and had packed them all. He had even brought me a liverwurst sandwich because I had written to him once that I missed the German liverwurst. I was touched by his gesture.

When we got home, Father and Gela were surprised at how well things were going for us. We had a nice apartment with three bedrooms, and we were in the process of moving into a large house so that there would be more room for all of us.

When we picked little Angie up from Mom's house, the joy was great! Gela loved my two little girls so much. Gela had not seen Sylvia in two years, and it was so much fun to see Gela and Sylvia, and Gela with the new baby, Angie. Even Father seemed to take to Baby Angie. Father seemed to be good with little babies.

My heart did sink, however, when Father opened his suitcase and there, neatly folded, were four sheets, several pillow cases and some handkerchiefs. He told me had had saved them for me. I just looked at them and took them out of his hands. I stood there for a minute, then thanked him for them and carried them into the laundry, the smell of the bunker in my nose. Here this poor man had lived fifty-one years of his life, and all he could show for them were those moldy sheets and a few pillowcases, which he treated like a king's ransom. I recognized some of them from when I was little. I tried my best to get the moldy smell out of the sheets. They were clean, but the smell was impossible for me to live with. I soaked them in hot water and Clorox, but that made things worse. The sheets were so old; they just came apart in my hands. I never told Father about that.

Father was pleased with the way I took care of him and Gela. His room was light and airy. Tony had painted it just days before they arrived. Gela and Sylvia shared a room, and the baby slept in the room with Tony and me. We bought Gela a youth bed and a pretty, frilly white comforter. There were so many things I wanted to do for her, but it wasn't easy on the salary Tony received as a clerk at the local A&P store. Tony never complained about anything I did for Father or Gela, though. He just took part in my happiness. That was all he ever wanted.

Tony's family liked Gela right away. They even liked Father. In my heart, I wished that things would always stay that way. I thanked God for the change that had taken place in our lives already. My happiness had no end. I not only had my sister with me, but I thought I had found my father. The good food and the good environment were agreeing with them. I could see Father had put on at least eight pounds and Gela even more. I remembered how Gela had looked the day she came off the plane. She had wanted to look grown-up, so she had worn nylons, but they had looked so pitiful on her, just hanging on her legs like the skin on an elephant.

Father had looked terrible that day too. I remembered how people had looked at them, but I did not care. I just hugged and kissed Gela, and I hugged Father. I noticed him backing off a little, not being used to affection, but I did not care. I had made up my mind that I was going to be nice to him whether he liked it or not! Deep down, I thought that maybe all he needed was a little love like everyone else. It seemed to work.

His attacks however, were getting worse, and he burned nearly everything in the house. He would get one of his attacks while watching TV; his ever-present cigarette would burn holes into the couch, the curtains behind the couch, and the new coffee table. I realized that he was not used to nice things, so I put ashtrays everywhere. One night, however, it was lucky that baby Angie's cries woke me up about 2:00 A.M.

I had gone downstairs to warm her a bottle, and by the time I got back upstairs, the hallway was full of smoke. I realized it was coming from Father's room, and I opened his door, smoke burning my eyes. I ran to open his window so I could clear the smoke. There Father lay in bed with a big hole smoldering where he had laid his cigarette next to him. I tried to wake him, but could not. By now, Tony was up, and he pulled Father out of bed. I could feel his pulse, and fortunately he was not burned.

Tony got the smoldering stopped, and the fresh air helped Father to regain consciousness. He told us he had woken up and wanted a cigarette, but must have had one of his attacks before he finished it and put it out. Tony talked with him about smoking in bed and how dangerous it could be because of the attacks, and, as far as I know, Father never smoked in bed after that. I still had to keep an eye on my furniture, though, but felt it was a small price to pay for the happiness of us all.

Now, with Gela and Father with us, my home in the United States took on a whole new meaning for me. Tony had tried so hard to show me his beautiful country, but I had been blinded with homesickness. Now everything changed. It was me trying to show off my new home and country to my father and sister. It did not take much for Gela; she loved everything. Father never spoke much.

We used to go for rides on Sunday. Maryland looked so much like my home. We went to Baltimore, which had the biggest indoor marketplace I had ever seen, called the Lexington Market. There were friendly farmers there, peddling their wares, much like the marketplace in Mannheim. Tony had taken a long vacation when Father and Gela arrived, so we went all over. We went to the zoo in Washington. Gela had never been to a zoo that size. We took a nice lunch and stayed all day. We put Sylvia and baby Angie in a piggyback stroller wherever we went; it could be easily collapsed and put into the trunk of our car, a 1951 Henry J.

I had done my homework about Maryland, so I could tell them everything about it. There was a population of 3,100,689 in 1961. We had the internationally renowned medical institution of Johns Hopkins University in Baltimore, only forty-five minutes from Frederick. The Chesapeake Bay, although a little muddy-looking, as we saw for ourselves, provided 400 varieties of fish. Baltimore also had a large petroleum refinery. Of some interest to my father were the rows and rows of fine Maryland tobacco growing. He had never seen that before. Both of them were amazed about the corn crop, since edible corn was unknown to German people. I was only too glad to tell them that I had just read in the paper that Maryland had grown about 28,000 bushels of corn that year, 1961. I told Father about the racetrack that was only thirty minutes from Frederick in Charlestown, West Virginia.

Then there was Washington, D.C. Frederick is sort of nestled between Washington and Baltimore, a forty-five-minute drive either way on the highway. Washington was the biggest attraction, with the Capitol, the White House, the Supreme Court, and the Lincoln Memorial with the statue of President Abraham Lincoln. Gela made me smile again when she said, "Say, Helga, wouldn't it be nice to sit on his lap?"

The botanical garden however, reminded me of home; we had had one in Schwetzingen. On we went, to the Jefferson Memorial, taking pictures of the times. Washington does remind one of Mannheim at its best—the well-kept lawns, water fountains, lovely buildings. It reminded me of the castle—the water tower, with its lion-heads staircase in Mannheim, but now there was just no comparison, because a lot of the buildings looked as if they had been built by German craftsmen.

Then there was our own little town of Frederick. I was so proud as I told them that our city was the county seat. Frederick had been settled about 1745 by Palatine Germans. It was the home of Barbara Fritchie and Francis Scott Key. I was also proud to show them the Maryland State School for the Deaf, Hood College for women, and Fort Detrick, an army post. (Fort Detrick is now being used for a cancer research center.)

I told Father and Gela that, when we got some money, Tony and I would take them to New York to see the Statue of Liberty. I told Gela that the statue had a plaque containing the poem:

Give me your tired, your poor,
Your huddled masses yearning to breathe free,
The wretched refuse of your teeming shore,
Send these, the hopeless, tempest-tossed, to me:
I lift my lamp beside the golden door.

We both cried as I translated the words into German. In my heart and soul, however, I thought, "Please God, don't let anything happen to this country and the wonderful people in it. Don't ever let there be a war like the one I had seen with its devastating aftereffects."

I remembered the huddled and the poor that day at Colmar at the train station. I saw the wretched refuse of our teeming shore. I had seen—and was—the hopeless. My heart and soul belonged to this country now. Sure, I loved and missed Germany, but my soul belonged to the country that believed in those words.

All too soon, Tony's vacation was over. I was so happy to have Gela here with us. We soon moved into our new house, a large, two-story home that wasn't fancy but had three nice bedrooms, a nice bathroom, living room, dining room, and kitchen. It was downtown Frederick, near Main Street, and within walking distance of everything, since Father could not drive a car.

Father soon found a job as a caretaker at the nearby hospital and Gela began school in Frederick, where a wonderful teacher took her under her wing. Gela loved school. Everyone was so nice to her, and she soon learned English. The best time of day, however, was when she got home after three o'clock and spent time with me and the girls. We had about two hours to ourselves before Tony and Father got home. She had become one of my daughters, and I was hoping that soon she would forget that terrible bunker.

I had never realized how deeply poverty had affected my sister Gela until one day, as I vacuumed her room. I saw a long line of ants making a path back and forth under her bed. I got a can of bug-spray, and, as I pulled out Gela's bed to spray behind it, I got the biggest surprise. There, neatly hidden behind her shoes, were all kinds of food: dozens of sandwiches all neatly packed in cellophane paper; cookies candy bars; and a banana, all black and rotting, which was the main attraction for the ants. I recognized the sandwiches as the lunches I had packed for Gela for school. I could not understand why they were under her bed and could hardly wait for her to get home from school.

When she got home that afternoon, I confronted her. She beamed with pride as she told me that she was saving that food for Tony, me, and the girls, in case we ran out. I just grabbed her and hugged her. My poor, sweet little sister, she was depriving herself of her lunch because she was worried about our running out of food! The very next day, Tony put up a large shelf in our pantry just for Gela, and we filled it with all kinds of canned goods, vegetables, fruit, and whatever we could think of to make her feel more secure. When she saw that, she was really happy. We kept that shelf especially for her for years. The only change would be to replace the older canned goods with new.

Life was really good for all of us—maybe too good to be true. It all started one Saturday when I left Sylvia and baby Angie asleep, with Father. I had taken Gela shopping with me, and Tony had gone to see his folks for a couple of hours. Gela and I were not gone long. I returned just in time to see Father giving Sylvia a terrible beating. I rushed in the house and asked him what had happened. What could three-and-a-half-year-old Sylvia have done that was so bad that she deserved a beating like that?

He told me that he had told Sylvia, three times, *"mache die Türe, zu,"* which meant, "close that door," and she had just laughed at him. I could see in my mind how he must have been talking to Sylvia and how Sylvia must have been lovingly smiling at him—her Papa—not understanding one word of what he was saying in German. I could see it all. She was just a happy little girl. Could he not see that she was just an innocent baby? My fears of him became worse, and justifiably so, as I soon found out. I decided never to leave him alone again with my babies or Gela.

One day, after Father had lived with us for about six months, Sylvia told me, "Papa Braun scares me." By then, I was expecting our third baby. It was due at the beginning of July, and it was now the end of April. I still had some hope for Father and us, and I tried even harder to be nice to him. I kept the children out of his way, and I even encouraged him to go buy a good-looking suit. He was still an attractive man, and I hoped he would meet a nice woman. We were willing to support him in any way we could. He was making a good salary; it was almost as much as Tony's. I thought that if he got a place of his own nearby, things would be better, but he would not hear of it.

Tony wanted to make some extra money before the third baby arrived, and even though he was working as a clerk at the A&P all day, he took a part-time job at a filling station in the evening. I really didn't want him working that much, but he wanted only the best for us. He worked three nights a week and some Sundays. That left my father alone with us more and more. Father always acted nice in front of Tony when they both had come home from their regular jobs, but now everything changed.

I remember well what started it all that terrible night. Tony had left for work that evening after dinner, and Gela was helping me do the dishes as Father sat at the kitchen table drinking a cup of coffee. Sylvia was running around in the kitchen, and baby Angie was in her highchair. Father was telling me, "Helga, why don't you let Gela finish the dishes and sit down?" I was already quite big; I looked every bit of seven months' pregnant. Not to cause any trouble, I did as he said and sat across from him near the kitchen door, leading to the upstairs.

I had heard that tone in his voice before, and I remember later thanking God that I had sat near the door. How well I knew that look on Father's face as he was saying how lazy Gela was, just like her mother. This wasn't true, of course, Gela had helped me quite a lot; he was just picking on her. I disregarded that look and answered him, "Father, I don't want to talk back to you, but please don't talk about Momma like that. I want my children to think only good of their grandmother."

All at once he hollered at me, "How dare you talk back to me!" and he lifted the heavy steel kitchen chair he was sitting on to hit me with it. He would have, too, if it had not been for my sitting on the other side of the table. I made a dash for the door as I heard the chair crashing down behind me, less than half an inch away from my body. I ran upstairs to my bedroom. I could hear him coming after me. I ran up the stairs as fast as I could, thinking how I had to protect the baby I was carrying.

I ran into my room, forgetting there was no lock. I pushed the dresser in front of my bedroom door, and it seemed as if history were repeating itself. I had seen how he had kicked and hit Momma when she was expecting Gela. I was not about to let that happen to me. I finally heard Father go back downstairs, and I just lay there on my bed thinking that he was never going to change, and here I was, twenty-three years old and still scared like a little girl. Anger swelled up inside of me, especially as I felt all kinds of movement in my stomach.

I thought perhaps I should not have said anything to him, but I loved my momma and Gela, and I could not stand by and let him say bad things about them. Gela had worked harder than anyone I had ever seen, trying to help me. I started listening at my bedroom door; it was so quiet that

I became really scared. I had left the baby, Angie, in her high chair and Sylvia and Gela were alone with Father. All kinds of terrible thoughts entered my mind. It took all the strength in my body to push that heavy dresser away from the door and go back downstairs. Just as I got to the bottom of the steps, Tony and Gela walked through the front door.

Gela had run out of the house the minute Father got mad. She knew what could happen, so she had gone and gotten Tony at work. Tony had dropped everything and came home with her. I didn't know where Father had gone; I guessed he was in his room. Thank God, Angie was still in her highchair, and poor little Sylvia was hiding behind her, trembling, but both of them were unharmed. Tony and I took them upstairs and put them in their beds, but it took quite a while to calm everyone down.

Tony found it difficult to believe what had happened. I had not told him about Father's bad tempers, but I had no choice but to tell him now. Tony wanted to talk to Father right then, but I told him to wait until the next day. Father was capable of hurting Tony, I knew, or even worse. It wasn't that Tony was afraid of Father; I just didn't want any more trouble.

It was a rough night, and, on top of it all, I started to bleed. I was just about frantic myself, but Tony calmed me down and called the doctor the first thing in the morning. The doctor told me to come into his office right away, and he saw me as soon as I got there. I told him that I had pushed a heavy dresser around (covering up for Father, as I had so often) and the doctor got really mad at me. He told me to go right home and go to bed and stay there, with my feet propped up. If I didn't want to lose my baby, I had better do as he said, which of course, I did. As I walked out the door, he called out, "And don't push around any more furniture!"

That night, I heard Tony talking to Father. He told him that he would have to get a place of his own. I don't think that Father understood him. Later, after I began to feel better, I talked to Father myself. I told him that we would help him to find a place. He never even apologized to me; again, he acted as if nothing had happened. He did, however, decide that he was going back to Germany, taking Gela with him. When Gela heard that, she said that if he tried to take her with him, she would run away. I assured her that, before that happened; I would hide her with some of my in-laws. I myself knew, however, that if Father wanted to take her, he could. The law was on his side.

I decided to beg Father to let her stay with me. That didn't work; he was determined to take Gela with him. When he started telling me how he had no money, however, I told him if he would return to Germany alone, it would be easier for him to make a new start, but he would not listen. Finally, summoning up every bit of courage I had, I tried one more approach. I said, "Father, I think I could give you five-hundred dollars to start fresh, but you will have to leave Gela with me."

To my amazement, he agreed to that. He knew he could trust my word; I had never lied to him. When I told Tony what I had promised Father, he was worried. We did not have even five dollars in the bank, and we were still paying back the loan we had borrowed to send for them, just six months earlier.

Tony and I went to every bank in Frederick, trying to borrow eight hundred, the amount needed for Father's plane ticket and the money for Gela to stay. We had a hard time since we already owed a lot of money then and Tony was just not making that much with four dependents. We finally decided to check out the local finance companies, and one of them finally lent us the money, at a high rate of interest. I couldn't help wondering what Tony was thinking of all of this. I'm sure he was not happy, already working two jobs, but he assured me that, if that was what it took to make me happy, it would be all right with him. He would do anything he could to restore peace to our family. He also knew it was too dangerous to keep Father with us.

Well, we bought the plane ticket for $238 of the $800 we had borrowed. Father packed his belongings in two large suitcases, having more than when he had arrived with only two small suitcases. I had remembered how important bedding was to him, so I gave him several good sheets, pillowcases, and handkerchiefs. We had also helped him to buy some clothes. He had a nice new suit, which he wore, several pairs of pants, and some of Tony's dress shirts. He also had new underwear, socks, and even new shoes. He had also bought some things from the money had had made from his job, such as cartons of cigarettes to take home. His suitcases were full and heavy when he left. (Father had not paid rent while he lived with us, but he had always given me money for groceries out of every paycheck he received.)

The five hundred we gave him would buy him furniture when he got back to Germany. That was a lot of money in Germany at that time. To make sure he would not change his mind about Gela, however, I waited unto the last minute to give him the remaining money. I finally gave it to him, in an envelope, at the airport. I started to cry as I gave him the money; after all, he was still my father. I was almost sure I saw him cry, too, as he turned around quickly and walked to the gate at the airport, but maybe I was wrong. We all watched Father's plane take off. Tony was holding baby Angie; Gela was holding Sylvia's hand. I just stood there, looking at the plane with tears in my eyes, the baby safe within my body.

So much had happened, but I guess it was all worth it, especially when I saw Gela and little Sylvia jump up and down with joy as they watched Father's airplane disappear into the sky, never to return, never to hurt them again.

My third baby was born July 2, 1962, a healthy baby boy. We named him Tony, Jr. Eighteen months later, on April 15, 1964, we had our fourth and last baby, also a boy, and we named him Rick Adam. My sister, Gela, lived with us until she met and married a very nice man. His family loved Gela too, and they now live in a lovely home with two little boys of their own. We are all very close and live near each other. There is never a week that we don't get in touch.

My promise to my mother was fulfilled.

The Forgiving

It was July 1967. I had not been to Germany in eight years. Living in the United States had changed me. Life was now so entirely different. There were never any serious problems; indeed, it was as if my former life had been a nightmare.

Before getting married, I made my husband-to-be promise that he would never beat our children. It was not necessary. Tony never touched our children. I personally only spanked our girls one time—the oldest, for running across a busy street when she was only three years old; the second oldest, for putting hairpins into light sockets. Even then, I only gave them a whack with my hand. I could never really hurt my children, not after what I had been through. I never wanted my children to live in fear as I had.

It's funny about children. The more I love them, the better they are. They seem to thrive under constant care, and, unlike Father's idea about using the rod, I believe that love and care will make a person good. My children are my pride and joy.

After my father had left for Germany, everything was fine. People even told me that I blossomed. Things went along well for a while, and then I came to the realization that I really missed my brother, Helmut. He had promised to visit me in the United States when he had money, and I hoped that he would immigrate and come live near us. I guessed he was unable to save enough money to come to see me, so Tony and I decided that I should see him. Things were much better for us now. Tony had been getting steady raises at work, and, since he worked at night, I was able to get a part-time job during the day. We took turns taking care of the children. We had also been able to put a down payment on a little tract house. It was small, but it had a huge backyard where the children could play. Our house before had been a city house and it didn't have a yard at all.

I had also just gotten my citizenship—with a lot of help from Tony. My sister, Gela, had also passed her citizenship the same day. We were so proud! When I applied for my American passport to visit Helmut, there were no problems. Now I could go.

When I wrote Helmut that I was coming to see him, he wrote me how happy he would be to see me again after eight years. He was greatly excited. He wrote that I could stay with him. So I bought my plane ticket and off I went.

Tony had taken a two-week vacation so that he could take care of the children while I was gone. I knew they would be in good hands. When the day finally came to leave, everyone wanted to see me off at the airport—all of the children and even my sister Gela and her husband. I remembered how the children had acted when Father had gone off in the airplane, but it was different with me. When I said good-bye to Tony, Gela, and the children, they all cried and told me to please take care of myself and come back to them. I just laughed, and reminded them that I was going for only two weeks. I have to admit, however, that it did feel good to have so many loved ones caring about me. Of course, I was going to miss them too, and I knew Tony was going to have his hands full with four small children, but I also knew he had the patience of a saint.

My sister's husband had insisted on driving us all to the airport. He had also promised to pick me up when I returned. His mother had lent him her station wagon, and we all piled in and off we went.

My plane was a Boeing 747, and in no time, it seemed, I was in Germany. As we landed, I looked out the window, and I could see that Germany—or I should say Frankfurt—certainly had changed. There was nothing left that would remind you of war. Everything looked so beautiful—the houses, the landscaping. Later, as I rode the train to Mannheim, I noticed the windows in the houses were full of window-boxes filled with flowers. Everything was so beautiful. My heart jumped with happiness. My eyes drank in all the new buildings, highways, bridges. Everywhere I looked, it was new. Germany had indeed rebuilt itself. I had heard that the American Government had lent the Germans money for rebuilding. I could see that the Germans had built themselves up and also learned that they had paid back their debts to the United States. I felt a little funny, however. I knew that I was an American citizen and had come to love my adopted country, but there was a spot in my heart that was very proud of Germany and its people. They had pulled themselves out of the mess Hitler had gotten them in and proved that they were good and proud people. I cried as I thought that.

A lady sitting across from me on the train noticed that I was crying and asked if I was all right. I told her of my thoughts. When I explained what I was feeling, and why, she said, "Did you know that Germany is the third largest industrial country in the world—after the United States and the Soviet Union?" She also told me that it had the second largest automobile production.

I did not know that Germany had recuperated so well. I had been so busy raising my family in Maryland that I had not kept up with events in Germany—at least that is what I had told her. In my heart, I knew that wasn't so. I had tried very hard to forget the nightmare I had lived through. My home now was in America.

It did not take long and we were in Mannheim. My first stop was at Helmut's apartment in Mannheim-Rheinau. I raced up the three flights of stairs and rang the doorbell. Helmut threw the door open, and, when he saw me standing there, grabbed me, suitcases and all, and picked me up and swung me around, just as he had done years ago. My suitcases and purse flew back down the staircase! When finally he put me down, we laughed and we cried as we retrieved my belongings from the second floor.

As we finally settled down on his couch in his living room, Helmut said, "Let me look at you." I had only been nineteen years old when we had last seen each other. Helmut had been twenty-one.

We just kept staring at each other. Helmut looked just the same even though he was twenty-nine. I was twenty-seven then. Helmut finally said, "You know, for a sister, you look pretty good, even though you are a little older."

"I can't stay nineteen forever, you know, and I do have four children!" I said.

"I'm only kidding. But you do look like Momma. That's a compliment, you know." I felt myself blushing as Helmut said that. I had really wished he would say that, and he did. Maybe he was just trying to be kind. I had always felt so ugly as I grew up.

We finally settled down for a long visit, and what a reunion it was! We talked until all hours; there was so much to catch up on. Helmut wanted to know all about Tony, Gela, and the children. There was so much to tell. Eight years was such a long time. Our letters had been our only contact.

We talked until 3:00 A.M. We talked about the good times, and we talked about the bad times. Especially the bad times. We both wondered how we ever lived through it all: the beatings, the starvation, the sickness, poor Strubele, Frau Katuck, Mother and Uncle Willi—we talked about it all. Helmut told me that Aunt Rosel was back in an institution and that Mr. Mannes had cancer. I did so want to see him and Aunt Rosel while I was home. I also wanted to meet and visit with all of Helmut's friends. I had all kinds of plans for the two weeks I would be there. Father was not included in my plans, however. I had not even written him to tell him of my visit. I did not want to see him. I just did not know how I would act or how he would respond, so I decided not to see him at all. I had made up my mind: I was going to have a nice visit, and nobody would ruin it. If I did not see Father, he could not hurt me.

I fell asleep the minute my head touched the pillow. In my dreams, I was a little girl again. I don't know what my dream was about; I know it was not a nightmare. It was something about Momma putting ribbons in my hair. It was the first time I had dreamed about Momma in years. When Tony and I had first been married, he often woke me up in the night to tell me I had been crying in my sleep. I got better over the years, but even then I still hardly ever had what you could call good dreams. It was a real surprise to me, then, to have a good dream about Momma. Her death had haunted me for years.

I woke up early the next morning and realized that I was back in Germany. As that realization hit me, all of the bad things that had happened years ago vanished from my thoughts. As I dressed, my mind wandered. I remembered one Christmas before Momma had died. She must have saved for months to scrape together enough money to buy flour, sugar, butter, and the other necessary ingredients for making cookies. My momma was the best baker in the world, and I loved and admired her so much.

She called the cookies *"Buttergebackenes."* Oh, they were so good, and they would melt in your mouth! She let me help her bake them; I was allowed to cut out stars, hearts, angels, and Santa's with the only four homemade cookie cutters we had. There was flour all over everything. I made a terrible mess, but Momma never got mad. She just smiled at me and said, "We'll get it all clean before your father gets home." A smile came to my face just remembering how we hid the finished cookies under the bed and how he found them the minute she went shopping and gave one to Helmut and me.

I also remembered the dolls Momma would make for me. They were made out of Father's old socks. She would use buttons for eyes and old handkerchiefs for clothes; Momma could do anything. When our old flannel sheets would get so thin you could see through them, she would make pillowcases from the good parts. When the pillowcases were worn, she would turn them into handkerchiefs or stuffing or clothing for my dolls.

I also thought of my beloved Uncle Willi, my mother's only brother. One year, he gave us a Parcheesi game at Christmastime. It was the only store-bought present I ever got in my young life. What fun we'd had—Momma, Uncle Willi, Helmut, and I—playing!

As I finished dressing, I heard Helmut stirring in the apartment, and before long I smelled coffee brewing. That also brought back memories. Since there was no coffee available during—or right after—the war, Momma used to roast either barley or wheat in the oven and then grind it in her coffee grinder and make coffee out of it. I can still remember how it tasted, and actually, at times, I wish I had a cup of it! Now, however, most housewives just go to the marketplace and buy a can of coffee.

Thinking of going to the store to buy coffee made me remember the marketplace in Mannheim. It was a large, outdoor market in the center of town, where the farmers would come to sell their vegetables and other items. They would be there every Monday, Wednesday, and Friday. Helmut and I always went to the market—not to buy, but to work. We didn't receive money for our efforts, but we always got some leftovers from the day's produce—sometimes eggs slightly cracked, cabbage slightly wilted from the sun, or apples that were partially rotten and soft. We didn't care what we got, Momma would always seem to work miracles and cook something good with whatever we brought home. I can still taste her *Apfel-pfannckuchen* fresh out of the frying pan.

It wasn't always easy for me to help the farmers load and unload their heavy crates. Sometimes it took all the strength in my small body. The farmers unloaded all of the really heavy crates and things, but Helmut and I still had to work hard. All of the effort and sore muscles were worth it, however, just to see Momma's face light up when we got home with our goodies.

As I stood there, what I thought about most of all was Mother's Day, 1948. Helmut and I had worked so hard to make enough money to buy Momma a present. We had earned exactly thirty pfennig. With our money, we bought Momma a box of "Suwa" (laundry detergent) and two candles.

The candles were the kind you would use for emergencies, such as when the lights went out or if you did not pay your bill. We used quite a lot of them. We were so proud of our purchase and so excited as we presented them to Momma with a handmade Mother's Day card we had made in school. Momma just looked at us with tears in her eyes and hugged us both.

That was the only present I ever gave to my mother. So many times I have asked God why she had to die when she was so young. Why couldn't she he here right now? I would buy her flowers and candy, and she could play with her grandchildren. One of my little boys was the exact image of her as a baby, blond hair and rosy red cheeks. Both of my daughters had her smile, and my oldest son has the ability to fix anything that goes wrong, just as she used to do. Momma would be so proud of us all. I know she would love my husband, Tony, who is the exact opposite of my father.

While I thought of my mother, an idea suddenly came to my mind: I would go to her grave and take her some flowers. It had been so long since I had been there. I asked Helmut to go with me, but he refused. When I asked him how long it had been since he had been to her grave, he gave me a sheepish look and admitted that he had not been there in years. I remembered that he had never liked going, not even as a little boy. I always went alone, even then.

Before I left his apartment for the cemetery, however, Helmut said, "I don't want you thinking badly of me for not going, but I would rather see Momma in my mind than in that grave. As far as I am concerned, she is in heaven."

It felt good to know that Helmut never lost his faith, even through the worst of times.

I tried to persuade him to go with me but finally gave up and decided that I would have to go alone. The cemetery was in Mannheim, which is about a ten-minute bus ride and then a short walk. There was a flower shop at the entrance to the cemetery, and I stopped and bought nine red roses, one for every year Momma had raised me. Clutching the roses to my chest, I walked along the graves and thought of all the times I had come to her grave site as a little girl. That was right after she had died. I remembered the comfort I had felt being near her and of all the talks I would have with her as I sat next to her grave.

As I approached her plot, my step quickened. I stopped in front of her grave and thought, *what is this? The wrong grave? I must be lost, but how could I forget where she is buried?*

It had been such a long time since I had been there; I assumed that I had made a mistake. I began looking for her marker. The more I looked, the more frantic I became. I could not find my mother! Finally, I gave up and found the caretaker to ask him for assistance.

When I explained what had happened, he looked through his records. "Lisa Braun?" he questioned. "Buried May 19, 1949?"

"Yes, yes!" I replied excitedly, "That's her!"

The caretaker just looked at me and said "I'm sorry, ma'am Are you a relative?"

"Yes, I'm her daughter. I just arrived in Germany. I have been out of the country for years."

"I'm sorry, ma'am. We sent your father, Adam Braun, three notices in the mail."

I just looked at him. "I don't understand. What do you mean?"

"When the family does not pay for the grave, it gets dug up after so many years. We are limited on space."

I could not believe what I was hearing! There must be some mistake! "What did you do with her? Where are her remains?" I shouted at him.

The otherwise friendly caretaker just threw his hands up in the air, not meeting my eyes, and repeated, "Ma'am, your father got three notices. They were all registered mail. I'm sorry." Then he walked away.

I just stood there, stunned, clutching my nine roses against my chest, my eyes burning as I fought back tears. I ran back to her former grave site and pretended my mother was still buried there. I gently placed the roses on the grave and whispered, "Momma, I'm back. I love you."

I don't know how long I knelt by her grave, pretending. Finally, I noticed people were watching me. It took quite a while, but finally I realized and accepted the fact that my mother's remains were not there anymore.

My thoughts and anger turned to my father. How dare he let this happen! He was not poor! Why had he not asked me for the money at least!? I would have paid it gladly! The tears of anger that I had been holding inside finally surfaced. Why had he done such a thing! Why had he done all of the things he had done!

Somehow, I made it back to Helmut's. I don't remember how. He was watching for me when I got there. When I told him what had happened, he could not believe it either. Father had never told him anything about it, but then Helmut and Father had not talked in years.

Helmut and I just sat there by the kitchen table, shocked, trying to figure out how this could have happened. I thought my father could never hurt me again once I left home, but yet, here I was again, torn to pieces.

Helmut came to my aid again as he had so many times in the past. Putting his arms around my shoulders, he said, "Remember what I told you before you left for the graveyard?"

As he said that, I remembered his words, how he would rather see Momma in his mind than in her grave. Helmut was right. Not only was our Mother with God, but she lived on in Helmut, Gela, and me. As long as we could remember her, she would live on forever.

After I left Helmut's, I went to see my father. Father still lived in Mannheim, and he was getting along fine on a rather healthy government check each month. He lived with his new wife, his fifth, in a nice, three-room apartment on the second floor. I truly wondered how long it would be before she would leave him. His first wife, Ruby, had left him. My mother, his second wife, had died. His third wife, who was the salt of the earth, had left him after years and years of beatings. I heard from neighbors that she had run off with an elderly gentleman who was almost thirty years her senior. I don't think his fourth wife, Hilda, who, he had written, was a very nice lady, had lasted more than a year before leaving. I wondered what his new wife, Gertrude, would be like.

When I arrived, Father opened the door. He was not expecting me, so he was quite surprised. It was with a rather uncomfortable smile that he asked me in. After he introduced me to his new wife, we all sat down in the living room. I really felt uncomfortable, and, just as I got ready to ask about Momma's grave, he said, "How about some coffee and cake? There is a wonderful bakery right around the corner."

With that he jumped up and left before I could say anything. Gertrude and I were left alone in the room. As we began talking, I realized that she was a wonderful person. My heart went out to her, wishing Father would be good to her. As our conversation got around to the past, she told me she had heard all about the things that had happened before she had married my father. She assured me that she married him because, as she put it, "There is a lot of good in him."

She painted an entirely different picture of my father, one that I had never seen. She told me that he would start to write me a letter, but then start crying and tear it up, unable to write me what was on his mind. I did not recognize the man she was talking about. My father cry? She must be mistaken. Gertrude proved me wrong.

"Wait a minute," she said "I want to show you something."

With that, she hurried off into the bedroom, returning almost immediately with a large wooden box which she gave to me. As I looked into the box, I was amazed. I just stared in disbelief, for there, tied neatly with white ribbons, was every postcard, letter, or picture I had ever mailed him. All the pictures of his grandchildren and me were in that box! What moved me most, though, were the two letters that were yellowing with age. One was written during a school trip I had been on back in 1952. The other was from the orphanage and had been written in November of 1951. In it, I had begged him to bring Helmut, Gela, and me home before Christmas. I remembered that he did.

"Those letters from you are your father's proudest possession," Gertrude said. "He takes them out time after time and reads them over and over. Then he carefully ties them up again and puts them back in their place."

I was still shocked. I never realized that my father cared about me or my letters.

When Father finally returned, we had an unexpectedly warm visit over coffee and cake. We exchanged father-daughter talk and had a visit that I had never imagined would be possible. For the first time that day, I saw a different man. I never mentioned the grave. In my heart, I forgave Father for everything.

That night, I remembered a lot of good things about my father. One incident that I had forgotten all about was the time my baby sister, Gela, had been put into the hospital when she was only three or four months old. My father and mother had been told that she was dying, and it was just a matter of time. Momma cried all day after they came home without her. That night, Momma told Father, "Adam, go and get Gela. I want her to die at home. Please get her."

It was in the middle of the night, but Father got up and brought Gela home from the hospital. I heard later that to get to her, he almost beat up two nurses and one doctor.

When he brought her home, she cried and cried. My heart went out to her, but I could not pick her up. Momma told me how much it would hurt Gela if I did, because she had large boils all over her body. I saw the boils for myself when Momma diapered her and it was awful; they were all over her back, legs, and everywhere. Momma tended Gela night and day, and Father was unusually good with her too.

I got a terrible scare one morning, however, when I saw Father sharpening his strop razor and holding it over a candle flame and then lifting up baby Gela. What was he going to do? To my amazement, Father lanced every one of her boils to allow the puss to drain out. Gela screamed and screamed, but I never saw my Father so gentle. When he finished, he put some ointment on the sores and gave the baby some broth. For the first time in a long time, Gela slept through the night without crying. It was a miracle, and soon Gela was getting better. Momma could not nurse her, so Gela had to live on dried milk, thinned oatmeal, and broth.

How could I have forgotten the way Father was with Gela during that period? He must have cared. I guess I only remembered the bad because I wanted to blame someone for all of the bad things that had happened to us. Now I feel sure it was the war that had made him the way he was. Sometimes now I wonder. Given the same circumstances, would I be kind? To what length would I go to protect my children from starvation?

I recently came across a letter Father had written to me when my children were still babies. In it he said, "Children are a gift of God." As I sit here writing this, it reminds me of a school verse, which, in German goes:

Kinder sind Geschenke Gottes:
Ihren zarten Körper pflegen
Himmelswärts die Seele weisen
Sei der Eltern höchste pflicht;
Den für Staat und für Familie
Ist der reichste grösste Schatz
Ein gesund und stark Geschlecht.

Translated into English, the poem reads:

Children are a gift from God.
To keep their tiny bodies clean,
their little souls toward Heaven, is
the parents' biggest obligation,
because for the State and for the Family,
the greatest wealth is a healthy people.

Epilogue

My brother, Helmut, died on October 8, 1970. It was only a few months earlier that he had come to visit me in the United States. It had been a wonderful visit. One day, just before he left, however, he told Gela and me something that upset us terribly. He told us that he would not live beyond the age of thirty-two. We were still shocked and devastated, however, to receive a telegram, just one year and three months later, telling us that he had been killed in an accident. He was thirty-two years old.

We had not really believed him, of course. I guess we did not want to believe him. Now we are not sure whether his death was an accident or not. So much had happened in our lives. Helmut seemed unable to handle it. He was never really happy, I could tell.

I, too, have had to shut my mind to some of the things that have happened to me throughout my life. Some things have haunted me all of my life and will always be with me. There are things I could never talk about, much less write about.

Writing this book is the hardest thing I have ever done in my life. I hope that putting my life on paper will release some of the fears I have felt and am feeling. I'm trying hard to live with my past. I know I will never forget it, but I'm hoping to learn to live with it, if only for the sake of my children. I would not want them to live through any of the unnecessary tragedies that I have seen. It hurt them terribly when their Uncle Helmut died; they had come to love him while he was visiting us, and we had hopes he would immigrate to the United States too.

Helmut's death almost caused me to have a complete breakdown. For two years after, my health was failing me. Finally, my doctor sent me to a psychiatrist. I remember that she cried when I told her some things that had happened to me.

That was in 1970. It is now May of 1982. I have learned to live with a lot of my memories, and many of my scars are healed. But I hope and pray that my children will never have to live through a war.

A Special Thanks

I would like to give special thanks to the wonderful people of the USA.

Sometimes I know all of you have asked what happened to all of those CARE packages, donations, clothes, and food, which you have given over the years. Well, I can tell you.

I was the recipient of some of those things after the war, when I was only a little girl. It was your dried milk and food that kept me, my baby sister, and my brother alive. It was your clothes that kept us from freezing to death. It was your medicine that made us well. Your generosity reached the right people.

I remember our minister telling us to stay after the Sunday service, and when he took us to the storeroom we found boxes stacked to the ceiling with clothes for the entire community. We were each allowed to pick out an entire outfit.

What a heavenly feeling to find a pair of shoes in my size with no holes! And socks, warm socks, that would keep me from getting any more frostbite. Then there was a warm coat with a hood. I wish all of the people who sent things to us could have seen me; it was Christmas in January! Only God knows how much we needed those things.

Most of all I remember finding that lovely red-and-blue plaid wool dress with a petticoat sewn into it, with lace around the neck and arms.

I asked my minister if it was all right for me to take it and he smiled and said, "Helga, I can't think of anyone more deserving."

I think it was the only time in my young life that I felt like a princess.

That night when I said my prayers I asked God to please keep those wonderful people across the ocean well and free from harm.

www.ingramcontent.com/pod-product-compliance
Lightning Source LLC
Chambersburg PA
CBHW022253290526
45785CB00015B/754